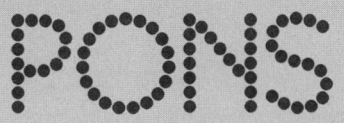

W0058737

MURDER IN THE FOG

Mörderische Kurzkrimis

zum Englischlernen

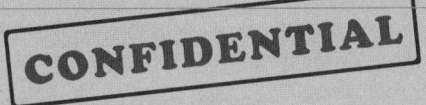

von Dominic Butler

PONS GmbH
Stuttgart

PONS
MURDER IN THE FOG

Mörderische Kurzkrimis

zum Englischlernen

von Dominic Butler

PONS verpflichtet sich, den Zugriff auf die zu diesem Buch
gehörige Vokabeltrainer-App mindestens bis Ende 2017 zu
gewährleisten. Einen Anspruch der Nutzung darüber hinaus
gibt es nicht.

3. Auflage 2016

PONS Online-Wörterbuch: www.pons.eu
E-Mail: info@pons.de

Projektleitung: Francesca Giamboni
Autor: Dominic Butler
Redaktion: Brian Wolfe
Einbandgestaltung: Anne Helbich, Stuttgart
Logoentwurf: Erwin Poell, Heidelberg
Logoüberarbeitung: Sabine Redlin, Ludwigsburg
Layout: Petra Michel, Gestaltung & Typografie, Essen
Satz: Datagroup Int. SRL, Timisoara
Druck: Medienhaus Plump, Rheinbreitbach

ISBN: 978-3-12-562778-9

Dominic Butler

Dominic Butler stammt aus Nordengland. Er ist Englisch-
lehrer und Schriftsteller. Nach seiner Schulzeit, die er an einer
klassischen Grammar School (entspricht dem deutschen
Gymnasium) verbrachte, studierte er Film und Literatur an
der Sheffield Hallam University. Während seiner Studienzeit
arbeitete er in Teilzeit als Gerichtsschreiber am Strafgericht
in Sheffield. Dort erwachte sein Interesse für Kriminalfälle,
die von nun an Thema vieler seiner Kurzgeschichten wurden.
Dominic lebt und arbeitet zurzeit in Italien, wo er Englisch
unterrichtet und gerade seinen ersten Roman beendet, einen
düsteren, jedoch humorvollen Krimi.

EINIGE WORTE VORAB…

Sie lesen gerne Krimis und möchten etwas für Ihr Englisch tun?
Mit diesen spannenden Kriminalgeschichten frischen Sie Ihr Englisch
auf. Die verwendete Sprache passt genau zu Ihrem Lernniveau, so dass
Ihnen das Lesen ganz leicht fällt.

Nicht nur Krimis lesen, sondern auch mehr
über Land und Leute erfahren:
Im Anschluss zu jeder Geschichte finden Sie
wissenswerte Informationen zu den **Schau-
plätzen**, an denen die Geschichten spielen.

Schwierigere Wörter
sind auf jeder Seite
in den **Fußnoten**
übersetzt. Im Anhang
können Sie nochmals
alle Wörter in
einer alphabetischen
Wortliste
nachschlagen.

Wo die einzelnen Schauplätze liegen, können
Sie in der **Weltkarte** auf den Seiten 6 und 7
nachschauen.

Alle Wörter, die in den Fußnoten übersetzt sind, können Sie
mit der **PONS Vokabeltrainer-App** üben. Gehen Sie einfach auf
www.pons.de/kurzkrimis-en und laden Sie die App kostenlos auf Ihr
Smartphone oder Tablet herunter!

INHALTSVERZEICHNIS
- -

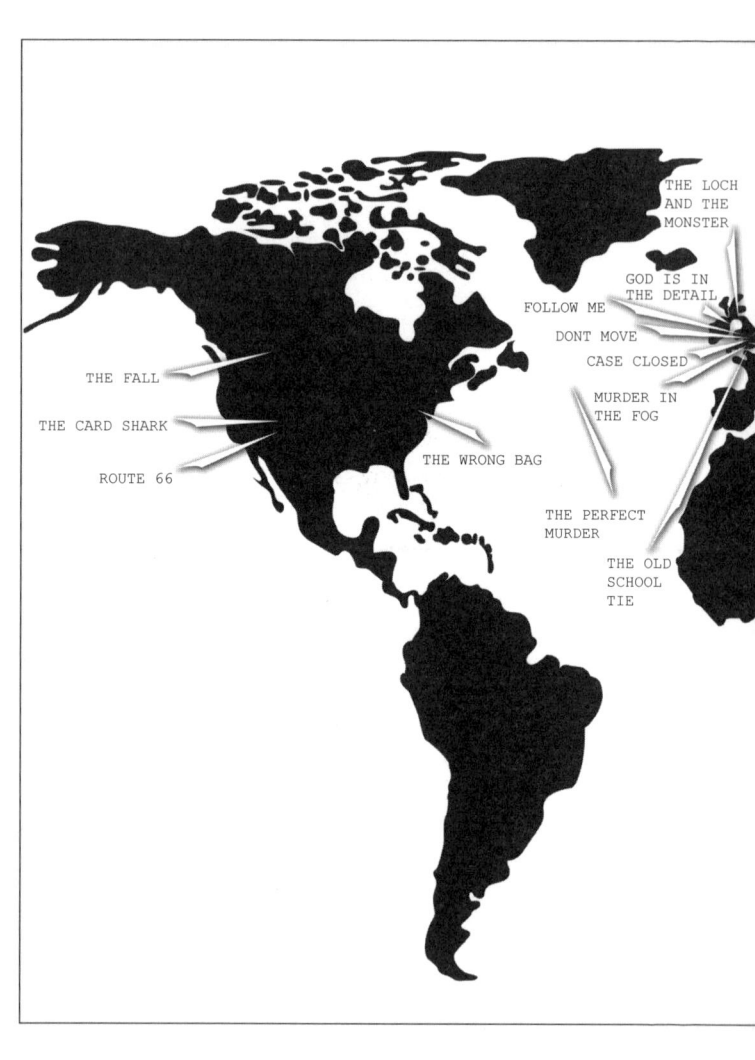

THE LOCH
AND THE
MONSTER

GOD IS IN
THE DETAIL

FOLLOW ME

DONT MOVE

CASE CLOSED

THE FALL

MURDER IN
THE FOG

THE CARD SHARK

ROUTE 66

THE WRONG BAG

THE PERFECT
MURDER

THE OLD
SCHOOL
TIE

ROB FROM THE RICH;
THE TUBE

THE POACHERS

HOW FAR IS
FAR ENOUGH?

1. MURDER IN THE FOG

I do not remember my name.

This is the first thing that I think when I wake, and I look around nervously, confused[1] by the dark and by the thick fog which surrounds me.

I raise[2] a hand to my face and feel a short nose and a small mouth. I try to remember my face, I try to remember the colour of my hair or what my eyes look like. I try to remember anything, but I cannot! I have no idea who I am.

I am on the ground lying[3] on cold grass which is wet[4] from the fog, and I am alone.

Why am I here? I ask myself, but I have no answer. I do not even know where this is because the fog is so thick that I can only see for a few metres in any direction.

I try to stand, but then I realise[5] that my head hurts and that there is a sharp pain[6] behind my right ear. I carefully lift my hand and touch the large lump[7] which is there. It hurts to touch, and I shout in the fog, the sound lost in the dark of the night. When I pull my fingers away, they are wet, and even with no light the blood is bright and easy to see.

I begin to feel more than nervous now: I begin to feel scared[8]. I imagine I can see shapes and figures in the fog, and I

---

1   **confused** – *irritiert*
2   **to raise** – *heben*
3   **to lie** – *liegen*
4   **wet** – *nass*
5   **to realise** – *merken*
6   **sharp pain** – *stechender Schmerz*
7   **lump** – *Beule*
8   **scared** – *verängstigt, ängstlich*

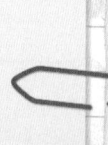

want to run. I feel that I need to run, that there is somewhere I must be, somewhere I must remember.

But before I move, I need to know something. So I push myself up and sit on the ground. I look carefully at my clothes, but they mean nothing. The jeans are new, but now they are dirty: muddy stains[1] cover the legs from the wet grass. The t-shirt is not familiar[2] either: just simple and black. So I empty my pockets, and at first there is nothing helpful there: no wallet, no keys and no phone. But then I see the picture[3], and I stop.

It is a woman, and even in the dark and the fog I recognise her. Her long blonde hair is beautiful, and her kind, friendly, blue eyes are perfect. Yes, I know her! And the thought is so strong that I smile despite[4] the pain in the back of my head.

But what is her name? I pull the last item from my pocket. It is a red serviette with a single word written again and again in black ink[5].

"Catherine," I say quietly into the fog, and the sound of my voice seems strange and cold.

Catherine. I am sure that I know her, but I still do not remember why. Is she my wife? My girlfriend? I think that she is, and I suddenly[6] feel afraid for her. "Catherine!" I shout into the dark, but there is no reply.

I am about to shout again when suddenly I remember something. I remember Catherine's face, but she is not smiling like she is in the picture, and her blue eyes look scared and desperate. I try to remember the image, and I see that there is a

---

1   **muddy stain –** *Schlammfleck*
2   **familiar –** *vertraut*
3   **picture –** *Foto*
4   **despite –** *trotz*
5   **ink –** *Tinte*
6   **suddenly –** *plötzlich*

piece of cloth[1] in her mouth so that she cannot speak and that she is tied[2] to a large grey stone by thick white ropes[3].

"No!" I cry out[4], and I push myself to my feet despite the pain in my head.

I do not know what to do for a moment. I only know that I must find her, that I must help her.

I think about the lump on the back of my head and the fresh blood on my fingers. Is there somebody in the fog? Somebody who has Catherine? Someone who wants to hurt her, who wants to kill her?

I want to shout again, but then I do not. If the person who has Catherine hears me, she is in danger. And another image comes to me. It is the face of a man. An ordinary[5] face with small dark eyes and dirty brown hair. There is nothing cruel[6] about the face, but I know instantly that this is the man that has Catherine, and I hate that face with all of my heart.

I begin to walk, slowly at first, unsure of the direction that I must go. It seems like the ground is moving slowly up, and I believe that this is right. The image I remember of Catherine tied to the grey stone is in less fog, and I think that it must be on higher ground.

I begin to walk faster, but I am soon running. The fog surrounds me, and the dark is without end. I try not to think of anything but[7] the direction I am moving in, but I am starting to remember things now. I remember Catherine. She has a black uniform, which she always wears at work in the restaurant, and on the uniform is a badge with her name[8]. "Hello handsome," she always says to me, "another day at the office?" And I never

---

1 **piece of cloth** – *Stoffstück*
2 **tied to** – *angebunden an*
3 **rope** – *Seil*
4 **to cry out** – *schreien*
5 **ordinary** – *herkömmlich, gewöhnlich*
6 **cruel** – *grausam*
7 **anything but** – *nichts anderes als*
8 **badge with her name** – *Namensschild*

say much, but I do not have to: we understand each other without words. And I remember that after I eat, I wait for her in the car park until she finishes work, and she is surprised to see me there. But I suppose[1] that's just who I am: a romantic.

Suddenly, there is a sound like a gun shot, and I fall. For a moment I think that I am dead and that Catherine is alone, tied to the grey stone in the fog. But then I see the light in the sky, and I realise that the shot was a flare[2]. I watch the light fall and illuminate the hillside[3].

Is it the man with the dark eyes and dirty brown hair? Does he know I am here? Good! If he looks for me, he is not with Catherine, I think. And I get up again and run faster now.

Do I hear voices in the fog behind me? I try to turn to look, but the fog behind me is too thick, and I only see the occasional light in the distance.

But in front of me the fog seems to be thinner, and I begin to slow. I am scared now because I know that I am near, and in the dark I begin to see large, grey stones standing like giants[4] on the top of the hill. In amazement[5], I think that I recognise this circle of ancient stones.

"Stonehenge!" I say.

"Yes," a voice replies, "and this is where it ends." And a tall man steps from behind one of the silent giants.

I expect[6] him to have dark eyes and dirty hair, but he does not. His hair is blond, his eyes light, and I think that this is not the man who has Catherine. Maybe he is his friend, his partner, and I am about to run when I see the small gun in his hand.

"I just want Catherine," I say, but I can see the hate in the man's eyes, and I know that the only thing I can do now is run

---

1	**to suppose** – *vermuten*	
2	**flare** – *Leuchtfackel*	
3	**hillside** – *Berghang*	
4	**giant** – *Riese*	
5	**amazement** – *Erstaunen*	
6	**to expect** – *erwarten*	

to the stone where I know she is tied and try to escape into the fog with her.

"Don't!" says the man, as if he can see my intention in my eyes, but I have to. At first[1], I think that maybe I am quick enough, but then I hear the snap[2] of the gun and feel the explosion in my back.

For a moment more I run, and I can see the shape of the stone where Catherine is tied, and I fall to the floor in front of it. "Catherine," I shout, but there is no reply. When I look to see why, I see that she is not there: the white ropes are still tied to the stone, but she is not.

"Catherine," I say again, smiling, because she is all that matters[3], and I can rest now because I know that she is safe.

"You got him, Detective?" a voice says behind me.

"Yeah, that's him," the tall man says. "He matches[4] the girl's description perfectly: dirty brown hair, small dark eyes. And look, the blood behind his ear is where she hit him before she escaped."

"Good for her."

"Yeah. We think she's his third victim[5] this year."

"So why didn't he run? Why wait here for us?"

The tall man is silent for a moment: "Who knows? I don't want to understand the mind of these psychopaths. I'm just happy Catherine is okay."

Catherine is okay. Catherine is okay. I do not understand anything else that they say, but I do understand these three words, and I smile again.

Catherine is okay.

---

1 **at first -** *zuerst*
2 **snap -** *Schuss*
3 **she is all that matters -** *sie ist alles, worauf es mir ankommt*
4 **to match -** *passen*
5 **victim -** *Opfer*

Stonehenge befindet sich in der Grafschaft Wiltshire im Süden von England und ist wahrscheinlich das berühmteste prähistorische Monument der Welt. Es stammt aus der Zeit zwischen 3000 und 2000 v. Chr., der genaue Entstehungszeitpunkt ist jedoch nicht bekannt. Viele glauben allerdings, dass die Anlage von Anfang an als Begräbnisstätte diente, da zahlreiche verbrannte Menschenreste dort entdeckt wurden. Wegen seiner Verbindung zu heidnischer Magie übt Stonehenge bis zum heutigen Tag eine große Faszination auf viele Menschen aus. Die Entstehung der Steinformation bleibt nach wie vor ein Mysterium.

2. ROB FROM THE RICH

The sun is high above Canary Wharf. High and hot, and looking down on the crowds of people[1] which wait on both sides of the empty road.

We are standing there, the three of us, in front of the bank. We are standing there in front of the glass doors, and no one is looking at us. They are all focused on the road, and in the distance I can hear the music and the commentator, and I know that the race is starting soon.

I look at our reflections[2]. We all have the same white and orange uniforms, the same caps, the same silver sunglasses. I almost[3] do not recognise the two men beside me, and I think that from a distance people cannot see that I am a woman.

"Okay, this is it. Ten minutes exactly. Remember your jobs, and remember: no real names. I'm Robin, you're Little John…" one of the men says to the other. "And you're Marian," he says to me, the only woman, and he gives me a quick smile.

Little John looks up. "The camera is still in position. It can't see us enter or leave."

I feel sweat[4] running down my neck.

"Here he comes. Remember the music, Marian," Robin says.

And then the guard is at the door, a short fat man who looks at us, smiles and then opens it without a single question. "You're quick: the air conditioning only broke this morning."

"We know," Little John says, "we broke it."

1   **crowd of people** – *Menschenmenge*
2   **reflection** – *Spiegelbild*
3   **almost** – *fast*
4   **sweat** – *Schweiß*

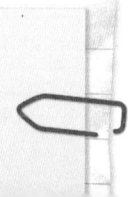

And the guard's smile disappears[1]. But it is too late: Robin pushes him back into the bank and John follows with the ladders[2] on his shoulders. I can see Robin's gun appear in his hand, and then I am inside too, and I pull the door shut[3].

"Music, Marian!" Robin says.

There is no stopping now, so I pull the small stereo from one of the black bags on my shoulder, and I press play.

Beethoven's Piano Concerto No. 2 fills the marble[4] stairs.

We run up the stairs together, Robin with his gun at the guard's back. Then Little John stops to cover the first camera. He climbs up the ladder in a second, and we run into the main room of the bank.

It is a large room with oak[5] tables, a dark marble counter[6] and expensive leather sofas. Behind the counter there are two women. "Out here! Now!" I shout at them.

To my left I see the short fat man sit down on the floor with his hands on his head; then Robin runs to the office and kicks open the door[7].

The two women move, but slowly; one of them looks down at the counter, where I know there is a secret alarm. "Not if you want to live!" I shout. "On the sofa!"

I pull two blindfolds[8] from a bag and cover their eyes. Then I tie[9] their hands, and I look at my watch. "Seven minutes!" I shout to Little John, and he covers the last camera with plastic.

I take a deep breath[10].

1	**to disappear** – *verschwinden*
2	**ladder** – *Leiter*
3	**to pull shut** – *zuziehen*
4	**marble** – *Marmor*
5	**oak** – *Eiche*
6	**counter** – *Schalter*
7	**to kick open the door** – *die Tür eintreten*
8	**blindfold** – *Augenbinde*
9	**to tie** – *fesseln*
10	**to take a deep breath** – *tief einatmen*

The music is so loud, and the bank, so hot. Can we do this? Can we really do this?

Then Robin leaves the office, and he has the manager, Mr Charles M. Hastings.

Hastings! I hate the name, and I hate the man. Tall, arrogant, dressed in his expensive suit[1] and with a watch that costs more than most people make[2] in a year.

"What is this?" he says, and he looks nervous but not nervous enough.

"What do you think?" Robin asks, and he tells him to sit at one of the tables.

Hastings looks around. "You can't be serious? A bank robbery[3]?" And for a moment he looks surprised, but then he laughs. "You idiots! This is an investment bank! There's no money here! Everything is done by transfer[4]." And he looks at us all like we are children, with that arrogant expression on his face. "Good Lord[5], you should[6] leave now before the police get here, and maybe you can still escape," he laughs again, "but I doubt[7] it."

Little John puts a blindfold on the guard. Only Hastings can see now, but we stand behind him. And for a few seconds there is only the sound of Beethoven as the music begins to reach its *molto allegro*.

"That's okay," Robin says, and he picks up[8] one of the bags and puts it on the table, "we brought our own money: twenty thousand pounds in small notes. Banks are difficult to rob. But houses aren't. Even big houses with alarms and safes. Like yours…"

1	**suit –** *Anzug*	
2	**to make –** *verdienen*	
3	**bank robbery –** *Banküberfall*	
4	**transfer –** *Überweisung*	
5	**Good Lord! –** *Du meine Güte!*	
6	**should –** *sollten*	
7	**to doubt –** *bezweifeln*	
8	**to pick up –** *aufheben*	

"What?" Hastings says, and then he looks at the bag. "My house? My money? You robbed my house?"

I can see sweat on Hastings' face now, but it is on mine too. I look at my watch. "Four minutes!"

"But… but what do you want? You have my money."

"Ha!" Robin laughs. "We don't want it. Not that: we're not common thieves[1]!" And he throws the bag to Little John. "Get it ready," he says, and Little John takes the ladders back down the stairs to the glass doors.

"Then what?" shouts Hastings.

And this is my part; I take the laptop from the bag and put it in front of him and open it, "Do you know what this is?"

He looks. "It's a bank account. A transfer. So?" he says, arrogantly.

"So we need you to enter your details and then transfer two hundred and forty thousand pounds to this account. Do it, and then we go."

And he looks more than nervous now. He looks scared.

"No! I can't, I don't have that sort of money. I can't… I…"

I put the newspaper down on the computer. "Really?"

He looks at the newspaper for a moment but says nothing.

"One minute!" says Little John.

"Read it!" Robin shouts.

Hastings is silent, but Robin points the gun at him. "Read it!" he shouts again.

"Okay, okay… Bank manager receives two hundred and forty thousand pound salary despite bank failure." He stops and tries to turn to look at us, but Robin pulls the trigger back on the gun. "You don't understand," Hastings shouts, "it's more complicated than that!"

---

1   **common thief –** *gemeiner Dieb*

"We understand that hundreds of local businesses are in serious trouble[1] because of[2] you and this bank," I say. "And you now have a decision to make because we have no time. Enter the details, or…" I say, and I know that this is it[3]. It has to be now.

Beethoven fills the silence again, and I look at Robin and see that there is sweat on his face too, but Hastings does not move.

"Then goodbye, Mr Hastings," Robin says, and he moves the gun, but…

"No! Please! Look…" and Hastings enters his details.

I do not believe it, and I take the computer.

"Well?" Robin says.

"It's done. It's gone. Direct. No one can trace[4] it!"

Then the music stops.

And I want to smile, but there is no time. In the distance I hear the sound of a gun, and the crowd outside cheers[5].

Robin takes the last blindfold from the bag and puts it over Hastings' eyes.

"And what now?" Hastings says. "You think you can just walk out of here?"

Robin laughs. "Something like that[6]," he says quietly.

"The police are out there. They'll see you. They'll stop you!"

Robin then puts his mouth to Hastings' ear. "Not if there's a big enough distraction[7]," he says. "Oh, and just to let you know[8], there are no bullets[9] in any of our guns."

Hastings starts to shout, but we do not listen. This is it, we have to go now. We take our uniforms off and put them in the bag.

1	**serious trouble** – *große Schwierigkeiten*	
2	**because of** – *wegen*	
3	**this is it** – *jetzt oder nie*	
4	**to trace** – *nachverfolgen*	
5	**to cheer** – *jubeln*	
6	**Something like that.** – *So ungefähr.*	
7	**distraction** – *Ablenkung*	
8	**to let sb. know** – *jdm. Bescheid geben*	
9	**bullet** – *Patrone*	

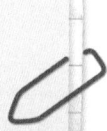

Then we are at the doors. Outside we hear the crowd cheer, and we see the first runners pass by[1]. Then there are more, many more, hundreds more, thousands more.

And now we start to smile, because we know we are nearly out.

"Now!" says Robin, and Little John presses the control on the air conditioning. For a moment there is nothing; then the fans[2] start.

And then money fills the air outside. Twenty thousand pounds. It flies over the heads of the crowd into the runners and into the road.

And then there is nothing but chaos.

And no one sees us walk slowly from the bank. And no one remembers us later.

And maybe you want to know what we plan to do with the money.

Unfortunately[3], this, I can never tell you.

ROB FROM THE RICH

---

1   **to pass by -** *vorbeigehen*
2   **fan -** *Lüfter*
3   **unfortunately -** *bedauerlicherweise, leider*

→ **Canary Wharf** ist Londons zweitwichtigstes Finanzzentrum, in dem viele internationale Banken und Finanzunternehmen ihren Sitz haben. Es befindet sich direkt an der Themse, in den West India Docks, und zeichnet sich durch seinen modernen Baustil mit verglasten Hochhäusern aus.

Jedes Jahr im April führt der **London-Marathon** 26 Meilen durch die Stadt, unter anderem durch das Canary Wharf. Mehr als eine viertel Million Zuschauer stehen dann am Straßenrand, um den rund 35.000 Marathonteilnehmern beim Laufen in der Frühlingssonne zuzusehen.

3. THE LOCH AND THE MONSTER

"No, Darling, she means nothing to me, less than nothing. I hate her. It's only you Emily, I promise... .What? Divorce her? That's impossible... Why? Because of the money, the house, the cars... No, Emily, of course you're more important than them, but... No! No, listen, don't go, listen to me, when I return to London, everything is going to be different... I have a plan, Darling.... Darling, I have a plan... Emily?" But there is no answer, and Oliver Stern puts his mobile back into his coat pocket and looks around.

There is no one near to him to hear. He is alone on the jetty[1], apart from the boat attendant[2] at his chair twenty metres away, his feet on a boat and a cigarette in his mouth. And he cannot hear from there, Oliver is sure. But just to be safe he decides not to phone Emily again.

Perhaps the less she knows, the better.

A plan. Yes, he has a plan, a good plan, and a simple plan.

He looks out across the horrible, grey loch[3]. The sun is almost down behind the green, snowy mountains now, and it is colder than before. "What sort of person wants to have a holiday in this remote[4], ugly part of the world?"

Then he hears the sound of his wife's laughter[5] from the terrace bar of the hotel, and he shakes his head[6].

"The sort of person like my monster of a wife."

---

1 **jetty** – *Pier*
2 **attendant** – *Wärter*
3 **loch** – *(Schottisch) See*
4 **remote** – *abgelegen*
5 **laughter** – *Gelächter*
6 **to shake one's head** – *den Kopf schütteln*

He tries to picture Emily: her eyes are so loving, her laugh so light and pretty. But when his wife laughs, she sounds like a donkey[1].

He looks at the loch again, at the jetty and the small boats waiting there for the tourists in the hotel. And he asks himself once more if he can do it.

"Ah ha ha ha ha ha ha ha!" she brays[2] again.

And he knows that he can.

It is ten-to-six now; the boats stop going out at six. And the sun is almost gone.

She needs to come now, he knows, but he cannot shout[3] for her. No, it is her idea to go on a boat. Everyone in the bar knows she wants to go. I just need to wait for her like a good husband, he thinks.

The type of husband who is happy to go out on the huge, horrible loch, in the dark, with his monster of a wife.

But can she still swim? He is not sure. He thinks that with her clothes and her coat on she will be too heavy and that the cold grey water of the loch will pull her down. But is that enough[4]?

He looks at the bag by his feet. The romantic picnic filled with all the food his wife loves. And the bottle of champagne that he knows she cannot resist.

Oliver smiles. It is a heavy bag. All he has to do is make her hold it for a second. Perhaps, quickly wrap[5] the straps[6] around her hands. Then…

No more monster.

But it is nearly six now.

The attendant is about to finish for the night.

1   **donkey** – *Esel*
2   **to bray** – *wiehern, kreischen*
3   **to shout** – *rufen*
4   **enough** – *genug*
5   **to wrap** – *wickeln*
6   **strap** – *Riemen*

"Excuse me," Oliver shouts with a smile. He pulls his cigarette packet from his pocket and walks over. "Sorry to bother[1] you, but do you have a lighter?"

The attendant has a hard face and fierce red hair. He looks at Oliver for a moment, nods, pulls his lighter from his pocket and offers it.

"Look," continues Oliver, "my wife wants to take a boat out. She's going to be here in a second."

The man looks at the sky.

"A boat, man, we want a boat."

"I dinna ken aboot that. Better the morra.[2]"

The idiot does not speak English, Oliver thinks. Bloody[3] country. "I'm sorry, I don't understand. I'm from England."

The man laughs, stands up and says nothing.

Oliver tries to stay calm, but he knows there is too little time. "Don't you speak English? My wife wants to go out now. She's only going to be one minute[4]!" he shouts, and the attendant stops and gives him a long, hard look with his cold, blue eyes.

"Oliver! Here I am!" a loud, cheerful voice says. And the two men turn to see Mrs Sylvia Stern. She smiles that stupid, cow-like smile at them, and Oliver sees the idiot attendant smile back. She is dressed in a horrible tartan[5] skirt and woollen jumper. And in her arms she has the heavy wax coat. Good, Oliver thinks.

"Darling," he says, with a smile, "this good man wants to close. I think we must wait until tomorrow now."

"Oh no, surely not?" She turns to the man and smiles again. "Can't we just go out for a few minutes, please? Just to enjoy the sunset?"

THE LOCH AND THE MONSTER

---

1   **to bother** – *stören*
2   **I dinna ken aboot that. Better the morra.** – *(Schottisch) Ich weiß nicht. Lieber morgen.*
3   **bloody** – *(AUS, BE) verdammt*
4   **She's only going to be one minute.** – *Sie ist gleich da.*
5   **tartan** – *schottengemustert*

And the attendant ignores Oliver but returns her smile. "Ay, well, just for 10 minutes then."

"Oh thank you!" Sylvia says, and the attendant helps them into the small rowing boat and passes Oliver the picnic bag. He then gives him another long, hard look, but Oliver does not care.

"Bloody idiot," he says to Sylvia as they slowly move away from the jetty onto the dark water. "I don't understand a thing he says."

But Sylvia does not seem[1] to hear and instead[2] looks out at the dark loch.

For five minutes Oliver rows[3], and soon the jetty and the hotel look much smaller, while the attendant is almost impossible to see in the half-light of the new evening.

And so this is it.

Oliver thinks about loving, ironic Emily again. Then he looks at his monster of a wife.

Oh yes, this has to be it. No more listening to that awful laugh, no more looking at her boring face. And, perhaps more importantly, no more sharing his bank account with her.

"Darling?" he says. "Shall we have a little drink?"

"Oh yes, that would be very nice!" She smiles, but in the half-light Oliver thinks he sees something strange in her expression.

"Can you pass me over the bag? Then you can come and sit here next to me," he says as casually as he can.

"Of course," Sylvia says, and she stands up, which makes the boat rock.[4] Oliver thinks that this is going to be very easy indeed. Just one push[5], and then he can shout for the attendant and pretend to help but really just watch the monster go down into the loch.

Just one look back at the jetty to be sure no one can see, he thinks, and he turns his head.

And then it happens.

---

1   **to seem** – *scheinen*
2   **instead** – *stattdessen*
3   **to row** – *rudern*
4   **to rock** – *schaukeln*
5   **push** – *Stoß, Schubs*

Pain explodes at the back of his head, and his eyes go dark. For a second he does not know where he is. Then he feels hands on him, pushing him and moving him. As he tries to say something, he sees the broken champagne bottle at his feet. Then he falls from the boat, and the ice-cold water takes the words and the air from his mouth.

For a moment he goes down, but then he kicks his legs, and he comes to the surface and looks up at Sylvia in the boat. She has an oar[1] in her hands, and she is reaching it out[2] to him.

"Yes, closer! Help me!" he shouts, and it is then that he sees the strange expression on her face again. "Sylvia, darling?"

"Don't you dare call me that," she says in a tone as cold as the water. "You're a cheating, lying, horrible monster of a man. You can call that stupid girl of yours 'Darling,' but not me. Never again Oliver Stern, never again."

And then the oar hits him on the head, and he cannot think, and he cannot swim, and the water takes him.

For a few moments he sinks[3] slowly into the great loch, but then, somehow, miraculously[4], he kicks again, and he comes to the surface once more. Sylvia and the boat are gone, and the half-light is complete darkness[5] now. He tries to swim, but his clothes and his coat are too heavy.

The jetty! The attendant! He has to still be there. If he hears me, he can bring a boat out.

"Help me!" he shouts into the darkness. "Help me, for the love of God, help me!"

And on the small jetty on the bank of Loch Ness, the attendant hears, he takes the cigarette from his mouth and smiles. "Sorry, Laddie," he says quietly to the loch. "But I can't understand a word you're saying."

---

1   **oar –** *Ruder*
2   **to reach sth. out to sb. –** *jdm. etw. hinstrecken*
3   **to sink –** *versinken*
4   **miraculously –** *wie durch ein Wunder*
5   **darkness –** *Dunkelheit*

Loch Ness liegt in den wunderschönen und weit abgelegenen *Highlands*, dem schottischen Hochland, und ist einer der bekanntesten Seen der Welt. Ob sein legendäres Ungeheuer „Nessi" wirklich existiert oder nicht, ist nach wie vor nicht bewiesen.

Was im See bewiesenermaßen lebt, sind unter anderem Lachse, Aale, Elritzen und Forellen. Loch Ness ist zu allen Jahreszeiten sehr kalt. Trotzdem haben einige Schwimmer die Herausforderung angenommen und den See der Länge nach durchquert. Der damals 19-Jährige David Morgan, der heute noch den Rekord hält, schaffte 1983 die doppelte Strecke (74 km) in 23 Stunden und 5 Minuten.

4. FOLLOW ME

"Follow me," says Detective Branwell with a sigh[1]. His shift[2] finishes in five minutes, but there is no one around in Howarth's quiet police station, and so he leads the woman to the first interview room and tries to suppress the image[3] of a pint of beer in the Black Bull pub.

The interview room is cold, the lights weak and grey, but he offers the woman a seat and hopes that this will be quick.

As she takes her coat off, Branwell watches her. She has long brown hair that right now looks a little untidy. And she has deep-green eyes that at the moment are tired and nervous and show something which he does not completely recognise.

"Right," he says, and tries to smile to relax her, "what's all this about, then? The officer at the front desk[4] says you need to speak to someone."

"I do," she says, and her voice is thin and tense.

"About what?"

She waits for a moment, uncertain, and then she takes a breath. "About a crime."

Branwell pulls his notepad[5] from his pocket and places it in front of him on the table. He has a bad feeling about his pint in the Black Bull pub. "I see," he says, "maybe you can tell me your name first. Your address too."

---

1   **sigh –** *Seufzen*
2   **shift –** *Schicht*
3   **to suppress the image –** *die Vorstellung unterdrücken*
4   **front desk –** *Empfang*
5   **notepad –** *Notizblock*

She puts her hands on the table, and he sees that her red fingernails are chipped and bitten[1]. "Jane Thornton. I live at Brow Top Cottage."

"Brow Top? Oh yes, I remember. You have that little red sports car, don't you?"

"Not now, no," she says, and she picks up her handbag. "Can I smoke?"

"No, sorry luv[2]: rules and regulations[3]. I can get you a tea if you like," but she shakes her head and puts the bag at her feet. "Then maybe you can tell me why you're here," he suggests[4].

Again she waits, and again Branwell thinks that he sees something in her deep-green eyes.

"There's a man who follows me," she begins. "Every evening. Every evening when I return home from work."

Branwell nods[5]. "I see[6]."

"No you don't. Every evening. Every single evening. For almost a year now. He's always there, Detective. Sometimes he's so close that I think he can touch me, and other times he's far away, but I still know that he's there. And Detective, you might think that I'm crazy, but I know what this man wants…"

"What?" Branwell says. "What does he want?"

She pauses for a second, and he sees her hands shake. "He wants to kill me."

Branwell says nothing but watches the woman's face. She is scared, very scared.

"Does he speak to you, this man?"

"No, never. And when I try to speak to him, he…"

"Yes?"

"He disappears."

Branwell opens his notebook and takes his pen out. "Where do you work, Mrs Thornton?"

"Miss Thornton. I work in Leeds. I have a small media company."

"In Leeds? Then where does this man follow you from?"

"From the station at Keighley."

"You work in Leeds, but you don't drive? I think your sports car can get you there a lot faster than the bus to Keighley and then the train to Leeds."

"I told you: I don't drive it. Not now."

"Right, so he follows you…"

"From Keighley. I see him at the train station sometimes; then he's there again when I get off the bus in the town centre here in Howarth. And then he follows me to my cottage."

"You walk from here to Brow Top, up over the moors¹ road? Every evening? That's a dangerous road, and it must be more than three miles."

"Dangerous, yes," but she does not say anything else, and Branwell continues.

"Can you describe the man?"

"Easily," she says, but again she pauses, and Branwell sees her turn quickly to look over her shoulder. "He's tall. With dark hair. His skin is pale² and his eyes cold. Dead," she says. "He has dead eyes. And they watch me every day, and I think that they watch me at night too."

Branwell feels a shiver³ run over his back. "You think that this man enters your premises⁴? That he enters your cottage during the night?"

"I do. Sometimes I wake, and I know that he's there. I turn on the lights, and I see nothing, but when I go to the window,

---

1   **moor –** *Heideland*
2   **pale –** *hell*
3   **shiver –** *Schauder*
4   **premises –** *Grundstück*

I can see him in the field. He stands there like a scarecrow[1] in the dark. And he accuses me… everyday… His cold dead eyes accuse me."

Branwell shakes his head. Is she crazy or just terrified[2]? "Miss Thornton, if this man enters your house, we can arrest him. But to do that we need evidence[3]. Has he broken a window? Or entered the property by force[4]?"

She lets out a laugh, a laugh that is horrible to Branwell. "No, of course not. There's nothing."

"And he never says anything threatening[5]? He never says that he wants to hurt[6] you?"

She looks over her shoulder again quickly and automatically as if she does it a hundred times a day. "No, he never says a thing. But I know… I know what he wants. I know what he wants!" And she begins to cry.

Branwell puts the notepad away. "I'm sorry Miss Thornton, but there's very little that we can do. Let me make you that tea. A nice tea to calm you down; then we can start again and see if there are any other details."

She seems to nod, and he stands up and goes to the door. "We need a better description, you see. If we want to identify the man."

"What?" she says before he can open the door. "Oh no, no, you don't understand, Detective. I know who the man is. I know his name. I know everything."

Branwell stops.

"You mean," she continues, "that if I tell you his name, you can help me? You can stop this?" she says desperately[7].

1	**scarecrow –** *Vogelscheuche*
2	**to be terrified –** *schreckliche Angst vor etw. haben*
3	**evidence –** *Beweis*
4	**to enter a property by force –** *einbrechen*
5	**threatening –** *bedrohend*
6	**to hurt sb. –** *jdm. wehtun*
7	**desperately –** *verzweifelt*

"You know his name?"

"Do you promise? You can stop it?"

Branwell does not sit. He sees that expression in her eyes again. "I can't promise, luv, no. But I can try."

She nods and bites her red fingernails for a moment. "His name is William Grey."

William Grey. Branwell knows the name. William Grey. And he remembers something horrible from more than a year ago: an accident on the roads across the moors. William Grey: a local cyclist and a good man.

"William Grey? Miss Thornton, William Grey is dead. He was hit by a car last year while he cycled across Brow Top road. We never found the driver, but William died instantly, they say."

"Oh I know," she says, and he sees that something in her deep-green eyes, and he thinks that he knows what it is now. "I know, Detective, because I am that driver."

Then there is only the sound of her crying to fill the cold interview room, and Branwell sits down again and picks up his pen and notepad. "I think you should tell me everything," he says, and he can see clearly now the guilt[1] that fills her deep-green eyes.

An hour later Branwell closes the door of the interview room and sighs. He does not feel any sympathy[2] for her. He cannot: not for someone who can do that. To leave someone on the grey moors to die. No, he cannot feel any sympathy for her, but maybe now she can find some rest. Maybe now she can forget the ghost of William Grey.

He walks up the corridor to the front desk and is about to[3] shout for an officer when he sees the tall figure standing at the door of the police station. He stops, his heart suddenly beating faster.

---

1   guilt – *Schuldgefühl*
2   to feel sympathy for sb. – *mit jdm. Mitleid haben*
3   to be about to do sth. – *im Begriff sein, etw. zu tun*

The man's dark hair is wet from the rain outside, his skin pale and his eyes cold and dead. It is him. Branwell knows it, but he cannot believe it.

"Do you have her confession[1]?" the figure says.

"What?"

"Do you have Miss Thornton's confession?" the figure repeats.

Branwell nods. "Yes. I do. She's in the interview room now."

The figure nods. "Good. Then it's over." And the impossible figure turns to leave.

Branwell still cannot believe it, yet the similarity is perfect. "Wait, Mr Grey, William, wait… I need to ask you…"

But the figure turns and smiles. It is a cold smile, but Branwell sees that the man's eyes look a little more alive now. "My name is Grey, Detective, but not William. My name is Matthew… Matthew Grey. William was my brother…" he says as he opens the door to the rain. "My twin brother."

---

1   **confession** – *Geständnis*

Howarth, ein schöner doch mysteriöser Ort, befindet sich in den **Yorkshire Moors**, dem Heideland der nordenglischen Grafschaft Yorkshire. Die Stadt ist berühmt wegen ihrer Verbindung zu den Brontë Schwestern, die viele ihrer romantischen Romane und Gedichte hier schrieben. Mit ihren Steinstraßen und malerischen Kirchen verzaubert die Stadt all ihre Besucher. Noch mehr wird deren Phantasie jedoch vom Moor angeregt. Meistens ist es in Nebel oder Regen gehüllt und wenn der Wind im Moor sanft zwischen den Bäumen singt, sind es nicht nur die berühmten Schwestern, die sich einbilden Geister zu sehen, die sie aus dem Dunkel beobachten.

5. HOW FAR IS FAR ENOUGH?

Gerry pushes open the door of the small Australian pub and steps onto[1] the terrace with a pint of cold beer in his hand. Inside the pub it is small and dark, and the barman is rude[2] and suspicious, but Gerry has to agree[3] that the view from the terrace is more than spectacular. Red, sandy plains[4] stretch out[5] in almost every direction, and only to the east are there thin, light-green trees that lead to the low, orange mountains.

Gerry smiles, sits down at one of the small, wooden tables and places his bag carefully next to his feet. The rest of his luggage is in the pickup truck[6], but not this bag. No, this one stays with him.

He takes a cigarette from his packet, lights it and lets the hot evening sun shine down on his bald[7] head.

The outback[8]. This is it. This is far enough. And for the first time in a week, Gerry relaxes and lets his anxious, pale face smile.

You do not steal from Big Jones and stay in London. Everybody knows that. And Gerry understands better than most people exactly how true that is.

No, you either get out of the city for life, or Big Jones finds you. And when Big Jones finds you, that is when you go see the world…

1	**to step onto** – *betreten*
2	**rude** – *unhöflich*
3	**to have to agree** – *zugeben müssen*
4	**plain** – *Ebene*
5	**to stretch out** – *sich ausstrecken*
6	**pickup truck** – *Geländewagen*
7	**bald** – *kahl*
8	**the outback** – *Hinterland Australiens*

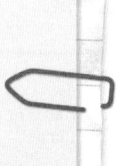

In little pieces.

Most people think it is just a story. But not Gerry.

No, Big Jones does not just kill you. He takes you to one of his old factories on the Thames[1], and then he shows you the boxes and the addresses of all the different locations in the world.

And then he starts to chop[2].

Gerry feels sweat run down his back. But he laughs and takes a long drink of the cold beer. Well, Big Jones cannot chop me up if he cannot find me, he thinks, and he looks at the bag at his feet.

It was easy to get it through customs[3]. They look for drugs and weapons. They do not look for sixty thousand pounds of uncut diamonds.

And he smiles and looks up at the hot sun.

"Well someone looks bloody happy!" a voice says, and Gerry jumps. He looks forwards but cannot see because of the sunlight. Then two tall, strangely dressed men walk into the shade of the terrace, one with three dead rabbits in one hand and a long rifle[4] in the other.

"G'day[5]!" says the other one.

They both look similar: messy blond hair under hats that are the same colour as their khaki shorts and shirts. And they are both dirty: their skin, boots and clothes all covered in red sand.

"Evening," Gerry says.

"Ha, a bloody pom[6]," says the first and drops the rabbits on the table.

"Is that right? Are you a pom, mate[7]?"

"A what?" asks Gerry.

---

1 **Thames –** *die Themse*
2 **to chop –** *hacken*
3 **customs –** *Zoll*
4 **rifle –** *Gewehr*
5 **G'day! –** *(AUS) Hallo!*
6 **pom –** *(AUS, abwertend) Brite*
7 **mate –** *(AUS, BE) Kumpel*

"A pom. You know, an English bloke[1]?"

"Oh. Yes."

"Nice one!" says the first before he disappears into the bar. Gerry is not sure, but he thinks that the man looked at the bag by his feet.

"Are you on holiday, mate?" asks the other, who sits down at the table.

"Yeah, something like that."

"Yeah, where are you staying? There are no hotels around here."

Gerry considers[2] lying, but Big Jones can never find him here. "Up at a farm at Hobb's Creek."

"Oh, is that right? Me and Darwin live near there! It looks like we're neighbours!"

"Darwin?"

"Yeah, my bloody brother. I'm Charles, he's Darwin. Here he is with the stubbies[3]."

And the brother called Darwin comes out of the bar with two small bottles of beer.

"The pom is staying at the old Hobb's farm, Darwin."

"Well you're no wuss[4] then. Be careful up there, mate. That's saltie[5] territory now." And both of the brothers smile.

"Saltie territory? What's that?"

"Crocs mate. Crocodiles. There are a lot of them up in the creek[6]. Best be careful." And they laugh again, and Gerry smiles.

"Yeah, sure, I'll be careful," he says. And he thinks he sees one of the brothers look at his bag again. "Well, nice to meet you both, but I need to get up to the farm before dark."

"Sure, mate. No worries!" says Charles.

---

1 **bloke** – *(AUS, BE) Kerl*
2 **to consider** – *überlegen*
3 **stubby** – *(AUS) Bier*
4 **wuss** – *Weichei*
5 **saltie** – *australisches Leistenkrokodil*
6 **creek** – *Nebenfluss*

"Watch out for the salties, mate. They can chop you up into little pieces," says Darwin, and Gerry thinks about Big Jones and the old factory on the Thames.

"I'll be okay. See you later," he says to the brothers, then he heads for[1] the truck.

"A bloody pom," says Charlie quietly.

"He seems to like that bag very much[2]." says Darwin.

"He sure does. You know, I don't think he believes us about the salties."

"Bloody poms never believe us about the salties."

And the brothers laugh as[3] they watch Gerry and the truck drive up the road to Hobbs Creek while the great Australian sun begins to fall behind the horizon.

It is almost dark when Gerry reaches the farm. The building is old but in okay shape[4], and he turns the generator on, and the electric lights start. For half an hour he unpacks his things; then he sits down on the terrace with his bag at his feet and lights another cigarette.

The creek is twenty metres from the farm house, and the evening seems to be alive with[5] insects and birds that live in the trees near the green water.

Salties, he thinks, and he laughs.

He does not believe the brothers, not for a moment. But just to be safe he pulls his new gun from the bag and checks it. Then he pulls a box from the bag, opens it carefully, and looks at the diamonds.

Beautiful, he thinks. Beautiful, and they belong[6] to me.

And he is about to laugh again, when he hears a noise from the trees.

---

1   **to head for sth.** – *auf etw. zugehen*
2   **He seems to like that bag very much.** – *Er scheint diese Tasche sehr zu mögen.*
3   **as** – *während*
4   **shape** – *Zustand*
5   **alive with** – *voller*
6   **to belong** – *gehören*

The box shuts in an instant, and then the gun is in his hand.

He thinks he sees a dark shape, but he does not shoot. "Who's there?" he says, but there is no answer.

He picks the bag up and puts it on his shoulder.

He takes a few steps towards the trees. "I've got a gun!"

But there is silence.

He tries to see what the dark shape is, but the evening light is too weak. He moves a little closer.

Maybe it is the brothers, he thinks, and he remembers the way one of them looked at the bag. Maybe they want to steal his bag. Well, they can try!

He raises his gun and is about to shoot when the dark shape moves again, and he laughs.

It is just a small crocodile. A tiny thing, no bigger than his arm. He looks at it and laughs again. "Well, you can't chop me into little pieces, can you?" he says to the crocodile.

And that is when he feels the knife at his neck.

"No," says a terrifyingly[1] familiar voice, "but I can, Gerry. Drop the gun."

Gerry drops it and slowly turns, the knife still at his neck.

"Big Jones? But… but… how?"

Big Jones smiles. He is tall and extremely muscly[2]. His face is bearded[3], and his eyes are full of violence and pain. But it is his teeth Gerry hates. Big white teeth as sharp as crocodiles'. "How? Do you think you can steal from me and escape? Gerry, you know me better than that."

"Please, Big Jones. I'm sorry. I have all the diamonds right here. Can't you let me go? You won't ever see me again, I promise!" Gerry begs[4].

---

1 **terrifyingly** – *erschreckend*
2 **muscly** – *muskelbepackt*
3 **bearded** – *bärtig*
4 **to beg** – *anflehen*

"I know I won't, Gerry, because you're going to go on a little trip… all around the world."

And Gerry remembers the old factory on the Thames and the boxes with the different addresses and the story about what Big Jones does when people steal from him. And Gerry opens his mouth to scream…

But the scream he hears is not his own.

The scream comes from Big Jones, who suddenly lets go of[1] the knife.

Gerry looks down and sees the small crocodile biting Big Jones's leg.

"Ha!" Gerry laughs, and he runs to his gun and points it at Big Jones, who falls to the floor and tries to kick the crocodile. "Don't move Big Jones. Let it chop you up into little pieces."

And Big Jones looks up at him and is about to shout when suddenly he looks behind Gerry, and the colour disappears from his face.

"What?" says Gerry.

And this is the last thing he ever says. Gerry's gun fires[2] three times into the evening light, and screams fill the creek, but there is no escape.

Soon all is quiet again, apart from the sound of three large crocodiles slowly creeping[3] back to the green water. Their big mouths now full of dinner. And of sixty thousand pounds of uncut diamonds.

1   **to let go of sth. –** *etw. loslassen*
2   **to fire –** *abfeuern*
3   **to creep –** *schleichen*

Die alte Verbindung zwischen dem **australischen Outback** und dem Vereinigten Königreich (England, Schottland, Wales und Nordirland) stammt aus der Zeit, in der Gefangene von Irland und Großbritannien in diese wunderbare neue Welt geschickt wurden, um ihre Strafen in der Sonne abzusitzen. Viele Gefangene starben sehr schnell. Die Menschen, die überlebten, wurden jedoch stärker und schafften es, sich den harten Bedingungen des neuen Landes anzupassen. Einfallsreichtum, Fleiß, Humor und Liebe für Sport und Natur sind Eigenschaften, die man noch heute als *typical Australian* bezeichnet.

6. THE WRONG BAG

The sky is not there.

In its place there are a thousand adverts on a hundred television screens, a sea of lights that constantly move and change.

Red, white, blue, green, orange, gold. Red, white, blue, green, orange, gold. They never stop.

And on the television screens there are giant faces, clips from movies, news headlines[1], commercials for cars and perfume, chocolate and beer.

The sounds never stop: the horns of the big yellow taxis, the music from the bars and the restaurants. And the voices. So many voices. So many, that they are impossible to understand. And so many languages: English, Spanish, Chinese, Italian, German, Portuguese. They all mix together and are little more than noise to an onlooker[2].

But the smells are the worst. One moment it is the scent[3] of hotdogs, onions, tomatoes, fries[4] or donuts. Delicious smells that make the stomach rumble[5]. But then it is cigarettes, alcohol, garbage[6] and vomit. And all of this mixes with the sweat of the thousands of people in one place.

Jake begins to feel sick again and looks down at his dirty old sneakers[7].

1	news headline – *Schlagzeile*
2	onlooker – *Betrachter*
3	scent – *Duft*
4	fry (French fry) – *(AE) Pommes*
5	to rumble – *knurren*
6	garbage – *(AE) Abfall*
7	sneaker – *(AE) Turnschuh*

Next to him Nick smiles. "You don't like it here, do you, kid?" he says. He always calls Jake 'kid', but he must be the same age as him: twelve or thirteen.

"It's okay," Jake says and looks up again. He has to be stronger, he knows; he has to be more like Nick.

"You're just hungry. After we eat, you will think this place is the best in the world. With a full belly[1] you can sit and watch this all day."

"It's just… well, why don't we come at night? Isn't it better at night, Nick?"

"How dumb[2] are you?" his new friend says, and he looks annoyed[3]. "At night they worry. At night everyone worries in New York. In the day, when it's hot and sunny like today, they don't worry about anything. They just watch those big screens, take pictures, eat and drink. They don't even look at us twice."

And Jake knows that he is right.

"Look. It's easy. You do what I say, no problem." And Nick looks at him for a moment: "You look okay now: these new clothes aren't bad."

The new clothes are not new, Jake knows: not really. Nick steals clothes from the washing lines on the backstreets. But they are better than the dirty old jeans and green jacket that are now in a bin behind the shop where they sit.

"You have to look good, kid. Remember that. You have to look like them," he says. "Then they don't worry. You can get near to them. Be casual[4]. Look up at the big screens. It's good if you get a camera out and pretend to take some snaps[5], you know? Then, when you get the chance… you do it… you grab[6] a bag. A woman's bag is the best: they have more things in them."

1 **belly –** *Magen*
2 **dumb –** *(AE) dumm*
3 **annoyed –** *genervt*
4 **casual –** *locker*
5 **snap –** *Foto*
6 **to grab –** *sich etw. schnappen*

But a guy's[1] bag is easier. A guy's bag you can just walk away with. If you get a woman's bag, you sometimes have to run."

Jake feels really sick now. The sun is somewhere up there, above the skyscrapers[2] of Times Square. And the afternoon is hot. The smells and sounds make a horrible mixture.

He thinks about home for a moment, but that is too far away now, and too long ago.

"You want to eat don't you, kid?"

Jake nods.

"And you remember where the cameras are? The NYPD[3] ones? The others are nothing. But don't let the NYPD ones see you, or you're not coming back here, not with me."

Jake nods again.

"So we do it now, and we meet back on Ninth Avenue. You got it[4]?" Nick says.

They both stand up, but before Nick moves into the crowds[5], Jake stops him. "But what if someone sees me? What if they stop me?"

Nick smiles. "No worries. Just say it's the wrong bag."

And then he goes, and Jake is alone.

He moves out into the crowds of people. He knows where he has to go: to the red stairs.

He moves slowly. No one really sees him; no one really looks. But he sees, he looks, he watches.

He sees kids his own age laughing and joking.

He looks at the food on the small tables in front of the cafes and bars.

He sees two policemen in the distance and he moves the other way. Walking between families and couples, businessmen and tourists.

1   **guy –** *Kerl*
2   **skyscraper –** *Wolkenkratzer*
3   **NYPD (New York Police Department) –** *die New Yorker Polizei*
4   **You got it? –** *Alles klar?*
5   **crowd –** *Menschenmenge*

When he reaches the red steps, he is hot and sweaty. Hungry too. But you can't think about that, he tells himself.

He needs to think clearly now. He needs to think like Nick.

On the red steps there is a group of maybe thirty Japanese tourists. They all have a camera and are all taking photos. But their bags are on their shoulders, and there are too many of them, he knows. Most do not see anything, but one always sees something, and one is enough.

So who?

And then he sees the man.

He looks like any other foreign tourist. He has a camera around his neck. Sunglasses on his face. And a map in his hand.

Except, Jake is not sure he is a tourist. There is something different about him. The man does not use the camera and does not look at the map. In fact[1], the man does nothing at all. Occasionally he just looks at his watch.

But the bag is by his feet. It looks expensive, made from black leather. Nick calls them weekend bags; he says they are the best. Inside them there are wallets, phones, tablets, everything.

Okay. Okay, you can do this, Jake tells himself.

He just needs to be quick. The man never even looks at the bag. So Jake begins to move in his direction, casually. He looks up at the lights and the television screens.

Then he is near enough, and he looks at the man. He thinks again that he is a strange tourist. From here Jake can see that he looks nervous.

But then the man looks to the right, and Jake knows it is his best chance. He grabs the bag and moves away. He expects to hear a shout, but there is nothing. So he moves into the crowds like Nick does. He wants to run, but he walks and notices[2] that the bag is heavy, really heavy. And he begins to imagine Nick's

---

1   **in fact** – *eigentlich*
2   **to notice** – *merken*

face when he sees the bag, and he already begins to imagine the food that he can buy.

But the bag is heavy, he thinks again. So heavy.

And he slows. Maybe he should look inside, he thinks, just to make sure[1].

He looks around and steps into the doorway[2] of a shop for a moment. Then he kneels down[3] and opens the bag.

And for a moment he does not understand.

There is no wallet. No phone, no tablet, no clothes.

There is only…

Then he hears the man shout, and he looks up and sees his angry face running towards him through the crowd.

He has no time to think, but he must. Can he leave the bag? Can he just run away?

Run away? When he knows what the man is going to do?

No. Not this time.

And then he is up and runs too, and he has the bag in his hands.

For a moment he has no idea what to do or where to go. He thinks that maybe Nick would know, that Nick would have some advice[4].

And then he realises that he does know.

And you remember where the cameras are? The NYPD ones?

Yes, I remember, Jake thinks. But can he get there before the man catches[5] him?

There is another shout from behind him, but Jake keeps moving. Above the crowd he can see the NYPD camera on top of a tall post, and he pushes past the tourists to reach it. For a moment there are people all around him, and he thinks he will

---

1   **to make sure –** *sich vergewissern*
2   **doorway –** *Eingang*
3   **to kneel down –** *niederknien*
4   **advice –** *Ratschlag*
5   **to catch –** *fangen*

never get there, but then he pushes past some kids who shout at him, and he is there. Directly below the camera.

And now? Now what?

He hears another shout, and knows that the man is nearly here, but the camera is not looking at him. It is turning slowly in the other direction.

"Hey!" he shouts, and he begins to jump up and down. "Down here! Look down here!" but he has no idea if anyone can hear him. He opens the bag for everyone to see, and there is a cry[1] from a woman near to him, followed by another and another. This must be why the camera turns. Jake holds up the bag, but he is scared[2], so scared, though he has to do it.

"That's mine," the man's voice says behind him. And there are more cries from the crowd, and everyone seems to know what is happening now. "Give it to me," the man says.

Jake looks at the bag one more time. What he sees inside looks just like from the movies: the clock, the wires[3] and the heavy packs of something horrible and dangerous. Jake wants to give it to the man because he is so scared.

But he will not. "No," he answers.

Then someone in the crowd says something, and the man looks around. The scared cries now become angry shouts[4].

Jake is pushed and he falls and loses the bag. He thinks that the people are shouting at him, and he wants to explain. But it was not the man who pushed Jake and took the bag: it was a policeman; the man is underneath four NYPD officers.

Jake now realises that the crowd is not shouting.

It is cheering.

1   **cry –** *Schrei*
2   **to be scared –** *Angst haben*
3   **wire –** *Draht*
4   **shout –** *lauter Ruf*

And a police officer helps him to stand and says something about him being a hero. "How did you know, kid?" a voice says, but this time it is not Nick.

"I... I... I didn't," he manages to say. "It's just... it's just the wrong bag."

Der **Time Square**, der manchmal als "Zentrum der Erde" bezeichnet wird, ist mit 39 Millionen Besuchern jährlich eine der meistbesuchten Touristenattraktionen der Welt. Er ist ein Sinnbild New Yorks, glamouröse Kulisse vieler Filme und Fernsehprogramme und viele würden ihn sogar als das Herz der Stadt bezeichnen.

Der Platz, der früher Longacre Square hieß, wurde im April 1904 umbenannt, als die New York Times dorthin umzog.

7. THE PERFECT MURDER

"The QM2, Darling, is the finest ocean liner[1] in the world. Sure, there are one or two bigger than her, but none of them has her romance or her luxury," Mrs Carolina Heath says as they enter the dining room.

Her young, new friend only smiles. She is a quiet young thing, and beautiful too, and Carolina likes to have beautiful things around her, so she is more than happy to talk for both of them.

"This is your first cruise[2], you say? You're going to love it. Just look at the view out there." And from the large glass windows they can see the majestic figure of the Statue of Liberty as the ship slowly moves away from the port of New York and heads into the deep of the ocean.

"It's fantastic," Eleanor says, and again Carolina is very happy to have a new companion[3].

The dining room is magnificent. The tables are covered in white, and the lights are low and atmospheric[4]. The band in the corner is playing soft classical music.

"Well, I wonder what the other people at our table are like. Oh my[5], look, here we are, table six. Well, good evening gentlemen." Carolina says, and the three men stop their conversation and smile.

"Mrs Heath," one says, "how good to see you again. Another evening of champagne and dancing?"

1	**ocean liner –** *Ozeandampfer*
2	**cruise –** *Kreuzfahrt*
3	**companion –** *Begleiter(in)*
4	**atmospheric –** *stimmungsvoll*
5	**Oh my! –** *Meine Güte!*

"Every night, Peter. My doctor tells me that I must," she laughs. "Gentlemen, let me introduce you to my new friend Miss Eleanor Chance."

Eleanor only nods and smiles.

"And these, Eleanor, well, how to describe them… I suppose every ship needs some pirates, and these are they. Meet Peter, Edward and Michael."

The men stand and nod politely, and Carolina is amused by the interested looks they give Eleanor Chance.

"Pirates?" Eleanor asks.

"Well, maybe not pirates, but you should still be careful. They are, in fact, writers, and I don't know which is worse[1]."

"Writers? How interesting."

"Please, sit down," Edward says with a smile that shows early signs of infatuation[2].

"No, I can't, I must find the captain: he promised to tell me all about the new people on board today; you know how I must know who I am sailing with." She looks at the men. "Oh, but can I trust you three to look after Eleanor? This is her first night, and her first cruise. She does not need to hear any of your horrible[3] stories or strange ideas."

"Oh, well, I suppose we can[4] change the subject, but we are having a really interesting conversation."

Carolina laughs. "I don't want to know! Just be nice." And she smiles at Eleanor. "If they scare you, just scream, and I can rescue[5] you."

"Oh, I think I can look after myself," responds Eleanor, and again Carolina thinks what a sweet, lovely thing she is. She must be only twenty-five or twenty-six. Her long blonde hair

THE PERFECT MURDER

1	**worse** – *schlimmer*
2	**infatuation** – *Vernarrtheit*
3	**horrible** – *schrecklich*
4	**I suppose we can…** – *wir können wohl…*
5	**to rescue** – *retten*

is elegant and her face full of classical beauty. And those eyes, such innocent[1], blue eyes.

Yes, a lovely, new companion, she thinks as she leaves.

At the table Edward offers Eleanor a chair, and Michael passes her a glass of champagne.

"So, are you all writers?" she asks.

"Yes," says Peter, "of different types. I'm in film, Edward here is a novelist and Michael writes plays."

"Fascinating," she says, and all three look happy that she thinks so.

"And what is this interesting conversation that I am interrupting?"

"Oh, we can't bore you with that. Please, tell us about yourself," says Edward.

Eleanor smiles shyly[2] and moves the elegant white silk scarf that lies around her neck above her black dress. "There is very little to say. I am sailing from here to Southampton, then I intend[3] to stay in England for some time. For the summer perhaps." Then she is quiet, and the three men think how polite and gentle she seems.

"I see," says Peter. "Well, this is a tradition of ours. Every year we take a cruise on old Mary. This is the sixth year. A good escape from editors[4] and deadlines."

"And wives," says Michael.

"Well, for them, not for me: I'm not married," says Edward a little too quickly.

For a moment there is an awkward silence[5], and Peter and Michael exchange a smile.

"Well, our conversation is about murder," says Peter to fill the silence "the perfect murder."

Eleanor smiles. "I see."

---

1   **innocent –** *unschuldig*
2   **shyly –** *schüchtern*
3   **to intend to –** *beabsichtigen*
4   **editor –** *Herausgeber(in)*
5   **awkward silence –** *betretenes Schweigen*

"I'm sure she's not interested, Pete," says Edward.

"Oh, but I am. Mrs Heath is lovely, but she only talks about scandal and gossip[1]."

"See, Edward, we can continue to argue!" Michael jokes. "You see, we all have very different ideas about what the perfect murder is. Peter thinks that for a film there must be something visual about the murder weapon[2]. For me the important things are the character and the motive."

"And for me," Edward says as he refills[3] Eleanor's glass, "the important thing is the twist[4]."

"The twist?"

"You know, the surprise at the end of the story, the thing you don't expect."

Eleanor smiles and takes a drink. The Statue of Liberty is still visible in the distance, but they will soon be alone on the dark ocean.

"You know, I think you're all correct. In fact, I have an idea for a story: an idea I think about occasionally[5]."

"Really?" says Peter, "Well you must tell us."

"Maybe," she says with another shy smile, "but you first: what's your idea for the perfect murder weapon?"

Peter laughs. "Okay, well, it's not my idea, and it's old, but I think it's great for a film. It's an icicle[6]."

The other two men laugh. "He always says this," Edward informs Eleanor.

"Because it's perfect. After the murderer kills the victim, they just watch the weapon melt. No fingerprints, no evidence[7]. What do you think, Eleanor?"

1   **gossip -** *Tratsch*
2   **weapon -** *Waffe*
3   **to refill sb.'s glass -** *jdm. nachschenken*
4   **twist -** *Wendung*
5   **occasionally -** *gelegentlich*
6   **icicle -** *Eiszapfen*
7   **evidence -** *Beweis*

She smiles, "It's very clever... but... well, I prefer fire."

"Fire?"

"Yes, fire kills, and it destroys[1] the evidence. And also a fire can look like an accident. The icicle never can."

"Ha, she's right!" laughs Michael. "So what about characters and motive?" he continues.

"A beautiful, young couple who are happy and in love."

"What, and he kills her?"

"No, she kills him."

"Let me guess: they're rich, she wants his money?"

Eleanor takes another drink. "No. She's the rich one."

"So what's the motive?" Michael asks.

"Wait a minute," interrupts Peter. "You say she kills him. With fire? How? She locks him in a room in a burning house?"

"No, because then he might escape. She drugs him with sleeping pills[2] during dinner. She always goes for a run in the evening, but this time she waits until he falls asleep in a chair in the lounge, and she puts a candle to the curtains. Then she goes for her run and makes sure that many people see her."

Peter nods his head, "Interesting, but a coroner[3] will find traces[4] of sleeping pills in the blood. They'll know."

"No, not with this type of pill. At a certain temperature it completely burns away. Only a small trace of it can be detected[5]. And if they are detected, so what[6]? They are his pills."

Peter laughs this time. "Excellent!"

"Very clever," Edward agrees, "but unfortunately the wife is always a suspect[7] in a murder."

1	**to destroy –** *vernichten*	
2	**sleeping pill –** *Schlaftablette*	
3	**coroner –** *Gerichtsmediziner*	
4	**trace –** *Spur*	
5	**to detect –** *entdecken*	
6	**So what? –** *Na und?*	
7	**suspect –** *Verdächtige(r)*	

"Normally, yes," says Eleanor, and all three men notice how her smile fades[1] a little, "but she has a plan for that. You see, she runs until she hears the fire engines[2]. Then she returns to the house. There are people there already, neighbours, and this is just what she wants. They try to stop her, but she runs into the burning building. No one follows her. They can't: they know it's too dangerous. And so she goes to her husband as the flames spread[3] over his body, and she watches. And while she watches, she lets the flames touch her, too. They reach out, and they burn her back and her neck and her hair. And at this point she screams and runs from the building and falls to the floor." Eleanor stops speaking, and for a moment there is silence at the table.

"My God," says Edward, "she lets the flames burn her."

Michael takes a moment to think about it and then nods. "It's perfect. The perfect way to avoid suspicion[4]."

"Everyone thinks it's an accident and that she is heartbroken[5]," says Peter.

"Yes," Eleanor says, and for a moment more there is silence again.

Then the band starts to play a waltz, and Eleanor looks at Edward. "I don't suppose you dance, Edward?"

And the writer goes a little red. "Actually, I do. Would you like to join me?"

Eleanor smiles, and they both stand up. She adjusts[6] the white scarf around her neck.

"But what about the woman's motive?" Michael asks.

Eleanor smiles. "Yes, that's the difficult part. And I'm afraid I just don't know. I suppose sometimes a person just… enjoys murder."

THE PERFECT MURDER

---

1   **to fade -** *schwinden*
2   **fire engine -** *Feuerwehrauto*
3   **to spread -** *sich ausbreiten*
4   **suspicion -** *Verdacht*
5   **heartbroken -** *untröstlich*
6   **to adjust -** *zurechtrücken*

And as Eleanor and Edward move away to the dance floor, Peter and Michael see her adjust the scarf around her neck one last time. And in the low, romantic light of the ballroom they both think they see something strange on her back and neck. Something which makes them stop and look at each other.

But no, it cannot be what they think it is.

It cannot be burnt skin under the elegant white scarf.

Can it?

→ Die **QM2, Queen Mary the Second**, ist der einzige transatlantische Ozeandampfer, der derzeit die Reise von Southampton nach New York antritt. Diese Reise führt über den oft stürmischen Nordatlantik - die gleiche Strecke, auf der einst die "unsinkbare" Titanic ihr Ende fand.

Die QM2 ist ein luxuriöses und romantisches Schiff, mit dem schon Adlige, Prominente und einige der reichsten und erfolgreichsten Persönlichkeiten der Welt gereist sind. Natürlich sind auch einfachere Menschen willkommen, die nicht im Rampenlicht stehen und dieses wunderbare, meisterhafte Schiff genießen möchten.

8. CASE CLOSED

Normally Nick likes his job, but not today. Today he just wants to get out of the hot courtroom[1], away from the serious lawyers in their black gowns[2] and white wigs[3] and go and enjoy the sun.

It is a good job, he thinks. It is better than serving drinks in a pub or helping out at his dad's office, but only if it is a short day, and only if the case is closed quickly. But today it is nearly three, and the case is nowhere near closed[4].

Still, he likes the title of his job. "Court reporter" sounds good; it sounds important, and that is exactly how he describes it to any girl that asks. In reality, however, all he does is press 'play' on the recording device[5] and write down a few notes about when the judge enters, when the prosecution[6] or defence[7] speaks, or what the final verdict[8] is.

And sometimes the cases are interesting, and he likes having some good stories to tell the guys in the pub. He also enjoys deciding who is innocent and who is guilty, but today that is too easy.

So he looks out of the window and waits for the judge. Sometimes he looks across at the defendant's[9] sister, a young woman with long, dark hair and sad eyes. But only sometimes, because the defendant and the rest of her family, the Lee family,

---

1   **courtroom** – *Gerichtssaal*
2   **gown** – *Talar*
3   **wig** – *Perücke*
4   **nowhere near closed** – *längst nicht abgeschlossen*
5   **recording device** – *Aufnahmegerät*
6   **prosecution** – *Staatsanwaltschaft*
7   **defence** – *Strafverteidiger*
8   **verdict** – *Urteilsspruch*
9   **defendant** – *Angeklagter*

are wild, and he does not want to make her, or them, angry. They have a terrible reputation[1] in Bristol, and there is not one of them that does not scare Nick.

"All rise![2]" the court clerk[3] says, and the jury, the lawyers and the family of the defendant all stand. Nick does too, and he remembers to press the button on the device. He forgot to do it once, and they refused to pay him for the day.

"Please be seated!" says the judge, a woman of about forty years of age with a serious face and tone. "My summary of this case is brief[4]. The jury knows all the details. On Wednesday the fifth of January Mrs Dawson went to the house of her sister, the defendant, Miss Lee. Mrs Dawson was bleeding from her nose and mouth; she also had marks on her face. She says her husband, the deceased[5] Mr Dawson, hit[6] her there several times. There are pictures of these injuries[7], but there is no proof that Mr Dawson hit Mrs Dawson. However, that is not why you are here. You are here because when Miss Lee saw her younger sister, she took a pair of scissors[8] from her kitchen table, said something to her sister and left the house. The words she said were 'I will kill him,' but the defendant says she does not remember that. Several people saw the defendant walking around Bristol looking for Mr Dawson. She stopped twice: once at the house of one of Mrs Dawson's friends and once at a local pub. Both times she had the scissors with her, and both times witnesses testified[9] that she said 'I will kill him.'

At half past two in the afternoon on the fifth of January Miss Stella Lee found Mr Dawson. He was leaving a cafe with

1	**terrible reputation** - *schlechter Ruf*
2	**All rise!** - *Bitte erheben Sie sich!*
3	**court clerk** - *Gerichtsdiener*
4	**brief** - *kurz*
5	**deceased** - *verstorben*
6	**to hit** - *schlagen*
7	**injury** - *Verletzung*
8	**a pair of scissors** - *eine Schere*
9	**to testify** - *aussagen*

a friend. The friend, Mr Harris, says that Miss Lee did not say anything to Mr Dawson and that the only thing Mr Dawson said was 'Hello'. Miss Lee then stabbed[1] Mr Dawson in the neck with the scissors, and he died in seconds due to[2] loss of blood. Miss Lee waited until the police came and was arrested.

Ladies and gentleman of the jury, you must decide only one thing. The defence says that this is not murder, but manslaughter[3]. They say this is the case because Miss Lee was not in a sane state of mind[4] when she killed Mr Dawson; they say that this crime was in defence[5] of her sister. The prosecution says this is not true. They say this is premeditated murder[6] because for half an hour Miss Lee looked for Mr Dawson; they also say she made her intention clear on three different occasions. Please, leave us now, and take some time to consider these events."

"All rise!" the court clerk says again. The judge leaves, the jury returns to its room to make a verdict, and the Lee family exit to wait in the lobby.

Nick sighs. It is obvious what the decision will be, but it looks like he will be here until four now. Cigarette time then, he thinks, and he leaves the courtroom. He has at least ten minutes; no jury can make a decision in less than ten minutes.

He takes the back stairs, passes three or four lawyers in their black gowns and white wigs and feels sorry for them: it is so hot today. Then he pushes open a fire door to his personal smoking area at the back of the court next to the bins and lights his cigarette.

The feeling of the sun on his face is good, and the taste of the smoke is even better. Tonight is a good night to go out for

1 **to stab** – *niederstechen*
2 **due to** – *infolge*
3 **manslaughter** – *Totschlag*
4 **in a sane state of mind** – *zurechnungsfähig*
5 **defence** – *Verteidigung*
6 **premeditated murder** – *vorsätzlicher Mord*

a few drinks, he thinks, and he is deciding whom to call, when he hears a female voice.

"Yeah, everything is fine, perfect... no, no one has an idea. Not the police, not my mental[1] family... of course it will be murder... What? Oh, who cares about her? She'll probably like prison, the crazy[2] cow: more people for her to hurt. And then I get his money, and you and I can get the hell out of this city[3] and out of this country."

Nick walks to the bins and looks around them; on the other side is the sister of the defendant. In the court room she always looks sad and confused. Now, however, she looks only victorious[4].

"Jesus," Nick says before he can stop himself, and the girl sees him and closes the mobile phone in her hand.

Nick looks at her for a second and then turns and runs back to the door.

He walks back up the stairs feeling confused and uncertain. He has to say something to someone, but who? The judge? Maybe.

He pushes the door to the courtroom open. No one is there. He moves towards another door and then hears someone else enter court.

"Wait," Mrs Dawson says, and she looks like she might cry. "Please wait: I need to explain."

Nick waits. Why not? What can she do to him in here?

She stands near to him, and he can see the tears in her eyes and the sad expression on her face, but this time he knows it is not real.

"I heard you. Your own sister? You wanted her to kill your husband."

"No, you don't understand. I don't know what you heard, but I love my sister, and I used to love my husband."

For a second only Nick waits. Then he shakes his head and is about to[1] turn.

"Look," she says, her voice different now, "I saw you looking at me yesterday. Maybe there is something we can do to make you forget this? Maybe you can take me for a drink." Then she smiles and takes his hand. For a second he does not know what to say, but he knows what to do, and he pulls his hand away and moves to the door.

For a second she is silent, but then she speaks again, though this time her voice is hard and angry. "Fine, go and tell them what you heard. Do you have any proof? No. So you can tell them what you want, but they can do nothing, and you are still here in Bristol, and so is my family. And they will not like what you say. Do you understand me?"

Nick stops. He understands, and she is right: there is nothing he can do.

"That's right, little boy. Keep quiet and you are going to be okay. I never hurt anyone; she did. Is it my fault she is so stupid? So easy to manipulate? A little bit of blood on my face, a few tears, a fake[2] story about him hitting me. It was so easy. And if you tell anyone, it is going to be just as easy to finish you. Understand?"

Then the door opens and the lawyers return, and Mrs Dawson's expression of sadness returns. Slowly they all come back in, and Nick knows he has to say something. He has to do something.

But there is no time, and there is nothing he can do. The Lee family is back in the room now, and he looks at them. They are savage[3], terrible people, who love violence.

---

1   **to be about to do sth.** – *im Begriff sein, etw. zu tun*
2   **fake** – *falsch*
3   **savage** – *brutal*

So, he moves back to his desk, and he sits down in the seat and feels defeated[1].

He wants to say something, but without proof he has nothing, and the judge can do nothing.

And he hears the door to the judge's chamber[2] open.

"All rise!" and Nick knows it is too late now.

He stands and is about to press the button on the recording device when he sees the red light flashing.

The red light?

The red light means it is recording.

It is recording…

It was recording…

It recorded…

"Stop!" Nick shouts, and he hands the recording device to the court clerk. "I think the judge needs to listen to this first," he says, and he looks back at the beautiful Mrs Dawson and sees that she is not sad now, and that she is not victorious, and not angry.

And he smiles at her because he thinks this expression suits[3] her best.

Yes, he thinks Mrs Dawson looks best when she is scared.

---

1 **defeated** – *besiegt*
2 **chamber** – *Amtskammer*
3 **to suit sb.** – *jdm. stehen*

Die klassischen Merkmale des **britischen Justizsystems** sind in der ganzen Welt bekannt: Weiße Perücken und schwarze Talare, ernstblickende Richter und Geschworene, die im Gerichtssaal sitzen, sind typisch für Großbritannien.

Basis des britischen Rechtssystems ist das Common Law, das auch in Australien, U.S.A. und Kanada angewendet wird. Das Common Law unterscheidet sich vom Civil Law, das in Kontinentaleuropa angewendet wird, hauptsächlich darin, dass es auf der Basis von richterlichen Urteilen immer weiterentwickelt wird. Auf vergangene richterliche Urteile, die sogenannten Präzedenzfälle, kann man sich für aktuelle Urteile berufen.

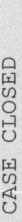

CASE CLOSED

9. DON'T MOVE!

It feels like[1] ice-cold water.

One moment you are asleep[2], your dreams calm and gentle and your body warm in the blankets of your bed. The next moment you are awake[3], a horrible sensation[4] filling your body, and you are sure that ice-cold water is covering you.

But it is not.

No, it is something much worse. Something that makes your heart beat faster. Something that makes the hairs on your arms stand up[5] and that makes your eyes search the horrible, complete darkness of your room.

No, it is not ice-cold water: it is fear[6].

And for a few moments you are so afraid that you cannot think. You know you are still in your bed, still in your house, still in your quiet street in the north of Manchester. And you want to tell yourself to relax, that everything is okay, and to close your eyes and return to your calm and gentle dreams.

But you cannot.

No, you cannot, because you know that everything is not okay. You know that you are awake because something woke you.

Some noise. Some movement. *Somebody.*

And you try to remember what it was, but you cannot.

---

1   **It feels like... –** *Es fühlt sich an wie...*
2   **to be asleep –** *schlafen*
3   **awake –** *munter*
4   **sensation –** *Gefühl*
5   **to make sb.'s hair stand up –** *jdm. die Haare zu Berge stehen lassen*
6   **fear –** *Angst*

So, you lie[1] there, and, you let your eyes adjust[2] to the dark. And you do not tell yourself to relax, you do not tell yourself that everything is okay, and you do not tell yourself to return to your calm and gentle dreams.

You tell yourself this: don't move!

The blanket of your bed is covering all of you except for[3] your head, and part of you thinks that this is good. Part of you wants to cover your head too. To hide, to be completely silent and to wait.

But another part of you wants to know.

Needs to know.

So you listen, and you look, and you try to remember what it was that woke you. A dog outside in the street? The alarm of a car? A baby crying in the next house?

Or something closer? Something inside the house? The sound of breaking glass? The noise[4] of the front door opening? A voice in the dark?

So you do not move, but you let your eyes adjust, and soon the complete darkness is not so complete. And you can see your room now, though[5] everything seems strange and different, and everything makes you feel more afraid.

The door of your wardrobe[6] is open, and the clothes inside look like three or four small burglars[7] watching you. The lamp in the corner of the room looks like the tall, silent figure[8] of a murderer, and the coat on the back of your door has hands that almost touch you.

But this is just your imagination, your fear, and you know that and try to stay calm and focussed.

1 **to lie** – *liegen*
2 **to adjust to** – *sich an etw. gewöhnen*
3 **except for** – *bis auf*
4 **noise** – *Geräusch*
5 **though** – *jedoch*
6 **wardrobe** – *Kleiderschrank*
7 **burglar** – *Einbrecher(in)*
8 **figure** – *Gestalt*

So you listen, and you think that everything seems to be normal. Inside the room everything is silent, apart from the slow and constant tick of the small clock on the wall, and the fast, irregular beat of your heart.

You try to see the clock in the dark, but it is impossible, and you think that it must be somewhere between four and six o'clock: the darkest hours of the night when even the lively and vibrant[1] city of Manchester sleeps.

Yes, outside the house the streets are silent. There are no shouts or loud voices coming from university students returning home from the pubs and bars. There is not yet the sound of the milk van[2] or rubbish collectors[3]. And there is no birdsong to let you know that the sun and the new day are nearly here.

You can imagine the street outside: twenty terraced houses[4] stretching down the road. Small houses, with neither rich nor[5] poor people inside them. All with tidy and ordinary gardens and ordinary cars. All silent and all dark.

You think that if you scream, someone will hear you.

But you are not sure. Not completely sure.

And so you wait, and you listen, and you look, and you tell yourself one more time…

Don't move!

After a few more moments, you begin to feel a little more relaxed. The street is silent and the house is too. Maybe it was only a bad dream that woke you. Maybe it was a text on your mobile phone. Maybe it was an animal in the garden.

And then you think of Sophie, your cat. But you know that the noise was not her. You know that Sophie is sleeping in her usual position at the top of the stairs and that she never makes a noise in the night, and you wish, for the first time, that you

---

1 **vibrant** – *lebendig*
2 **van** – *Lieferwagen*
3 **rubbish collector** – *Müllabfuhrwagen*
4 **terraced house** – *Reihenhaus*
5 **neither… nor** – *weder… noch*

also had a dog. A large brave[1] dog to bark and growl[2] at any intruders[3]. Yes, a brave dog to protect you instead of just a lazy[4] cat that lies in dangerous places.

And you almost smile, and you relax a little more.

It was just a bad dream, you think. And your heart slows, and the sensation of ice-cold fear begins to leave you.

And now you move. You pull the covers down to your chest[5] and make yourself comfortable again. And you know that you can rest now: everything is okay. And your eyes close, and you feel sleep begin to take you.

And then you hear it!

There! A sound! Not a dream, but movement in the spare room[6], where you keep the computer!

Don't move! Part of you says, the part that feels the sensation of cold water on your skin again.

But there is another part of you now, and it is not cold with fear: it is hot. Hot with anger. Because you know now that someone is in your house.

A burglar! Someone is here to steal your things!

Don't move! Part of you says again.

But you do.

Quietly, you move the blankets from your body, and you take the dressing gown[7] from the end of your bed and put it on. You know you should call the police, but you need to do something more, something quick.

At the side of your bed, there is a table, and on the table there is a small statue. It is a statue of a woman, and it is your favourite statue.

1	**brave** – *mutig*
2	**to growl** – *anknurren*
3	**intruder** – *Einbrecher(in)*
4	**lazy** – *faul*
5	**chest** – *Brust*
6	**spare room** – *Gästezimmer*
7	**dressing gown** – *Bademantel*

It is also a very heavy statue.

You pick it up, hold it like a club[1] and swing[2] it.

Yes, it is heavy enough. One hit to the head.

But can you do it? Can you hit someone? Can you hit a burglar?

Then you hear another noise from the spare room.

My computer, you think. My new computer.

And then you know that yes, you can do it if you need to. If you have to[3]. If there is someone in the next room trying to steal your new computer. Someone who thinks they can enter your house in the middle of the night!

What if there are two people? Two burglars? Or three?

Don't move! The scared[4] part of you says.

But you must. You walk silently to the door of your room. You quietly open it, just a little, just so you can see the dark landing[5].

Now you can hear the movement more easily. There are no voices. No reason for you to think that there is more than one burglar. You open the door a little more and step out onto the landing. It is colder here, but you do not feel it. Your heart is beating so fast that you do not feel anything but the strange mixture of fear and anger.

You move quietly, your back to the wall. The light switch is not near your door but halfway to the stairs. The door to the spare room is half open, and you can hear the sound of the wind outside. You know now that the window to the spare room is open, and you know this is how the burglar entered.

You take one more step to the door. Your hand is nearly on the light switch when you hear another noise from the room. Then the door begins to open slowly and quietly. You want to

1 **club** – *Knüppel*
2 **to swing** – *schwingen*
3 **If you have to.** – *Wenn du musst.*
4 **scared** – *verängstigt*
5 **landing** – *Treppenabsatz*

turn back and run to your room and hide under the blanket and be completely silent and not move.

But this is your house, and you know you must stay!

Then, standing right in front of you in the dark, you see the burglar, and he looks back at you and shouts. You turn on the lights and swing the heavy statue in his direction, but you cannot see him now because the light is so bright. You hear your new computer fall to the floor and break, and the burglar shouts again.

And then you can see his face, and you realise[1] that he looks more afraid than you do, and he is stepping quickly backwards to the stairs. He is young: just a kid, just a stupid kid…

Then you see Sophie, in her normal place at the top of the stairs, and you see how near the burglar is. You only have time to shout two words…

"Don't move!"

But it is too late, and he does move…

And then he falls.

---

1   **to realise –** *feststellen*

Im 19. Jahrhundert begann **Manchester** sich explosionsartig zu vergrößern, vor allem aufgrund der Textilindustrie. Diese erlebte mit der industriellen Revolution einen Boom und machte Manchester zur ersten industrialisierten Stadt der Welt.

Daher ist es kein Zufall, dass ausgerechnet Manchester der Geburtsort der Suffragetten-Bewegung (der Frauenbewegung, die für das Frauenwahlrecht kämpfte) innerhalb des Vereinigten Königreichs war und dass Karl Marx und Friedrich Engels hier begonnen haben, das Kommunistische Manifest zu schreiben.

Manchester ist heute eine der wirtschaftsstärksten Regionen Großbritanniens und gemessen am Bruttosozialprodukt belegt es hinter London und Birmingham den dritten Platz in England.

10. G O D   I S   I N
T H E   D E T A I L

The backstreets of Dublin are quiet, and the sun is slowly setting[1] on the old city.

Barry Brennan stands in the doorway of an empty shop and waits. He smokes his cigarettes continuously and enjoys the taste of each one. He enjoys another, sweeter taste, too: the taste of freedom.

But he has to be careful. He knows that. The gardai[2] are everywhere, and they are looking for him. And if he wants to keep his freedom, he has to be clever; he has to be patient.

And so he watches the street and the small redbrick houses. Most importantly, though, he watches the church.

His own parish church[3], the church of his childhood, Saint Anthony's.

How long ago was his last visit to this cold stone building? More than twenty years?

Well, that is not important at the moment. No, the only thing that is important is something that the church can offer him right now. The one thing he needs if he wants to keep his freedom and get the suitcase that is buried[4] in his brother's old garage. The suitcase that can help him escape the country and live the rest of his life on a tropical island in the Bahamas.

Sanctuary[5].

---

1   **the sun sets** – *die Sonne geht unter*
2   **gardai** – *die irische Polizei*
3   **parish church** – *Pfarrkirche*
4   **buried** – *begraben*
5   **sanctuary** – *Zuflucht*

And so he waits, and the evening becomes darker, and he thinks that there are now only one or two people left in the small old church. He decides that it is time.

He pulls the collar[1] of his stolen coat up to cover his face, and he checks that no one can see the grey prison uniform that he is still wearing beneath[2] it.

He finishes his last cigarette and stops to listen. In the distance he can hear the siren of a gardai car in the city centre, but he is sure it is not for him. So he crosses the road slowly and casually, walks up the stone steps of the church and looks around once more before he pushes open the wooden doors and goes inside.

Saint Anthony's. It smells no different, he thinks as he enters. And it looks identical too. The same cold grey walls, the same uncomfortable heavy pews[3] and the same weak candles to light up the dark room.

He was right: there are a few people inside. Two women sitting together on the front pew, their eyes closed and heads down. And an old man who looks at Barry for a moment before returning to his prayers. But not one of them is interested in him.

Good, Barry thinks: the place is practically empty.

He looks to the right wall and sees what he is looking for[4]: a large wooden[5] box with two doors.

Quietly he walks past the pews and stops near the box. He pauses for a moment to try and remember what he has to do next, but then the door to the church opens again, and three women enter. As he does not want them to see his face, he pulls open the left door to the box and enters.

A confessional[6]. As soon as he is inside, he hates it. It is small, so small, and it reminds him of his prison cell back in

1   **collar –** *Kragen*
2   **beneath –** *darunter*
3   **pew –** *Kirchenbank*
4   **to look for sth. –** *nach etw. suchen*
5   **wooden –** *hölzern*
6   **confessional –** *Beichtstuhl*

The Joy. "Father?" he says, but there is no reply, and he can see no movement behind the grille[1] that separates[2] his small space from the other.

So he tries to make himself comfortable on the small chair. But after a few minutes he realises how tired he is, and he thinks that maybe he can close his eyes for a moment and even rest his head against the grille.

But he mustn't sleep, he tells himself. He mustn't…

But he does.

And he dreams of the suitcase buried under his brother's old garage, and he dreams of the money inside and the paradise in the Bahamas.

"Hello?" says a voice, and Barry wakes up and looks around in confusion and fear. "Is there someone there?" says the voice.

Barry remembers where he is. "Yes, I'm here," he says, and for a moment there is silence before he remembers what to say. "Bless me, Father, for I have sinned[3]."

And again there is a long silence. Barry tries to see the face through the grille, but there is only a dark shape.

Finally the voice replies. "I see. Go on."

"First Father, I need to know something. I need to know that anything I say here is not to be repeated. That's how this works, isn't it?"

"That is true… my son," the voice says, and Barry thinks that it is a calm and honest[4] voice.

"Is that Father O'Connor?" he asks, remembering his old priest.

"O'Connor? No, son, my name is Keane. I believe Father O'Connor passed away[5] nearly ten years ago."

1   **grille –** *Gitter*
2   **to separate –** *trennen*
3   **Bless me, Father, for I have sinned. –** *Vergib mir, Vater, denn ich habe gesündigt.*
4   **honest (1) –** *ehrlich*
5   **to pass away –** *entschlafen*

Barry nods in the dark space. "But does it matter that you're not my priest? Can you still listen?"

"Any man can listen," says the quiet voice.

"But can you promise[1] not to tell anyone?"

"I promise, my son, I will not tell a soul[2]."

And Barry nods again and feels ready to speak. "Father, I need to ask for something from you. I need to ask for sanctuary."

"Sanctuary?"

"Yes, Father, I need somewhere to hide for a few days, a week maybe. Can you do that? Can you help me hide here in the church?"

There is another silence. "Maybe, but why, my son? I can only help you if you tell me why. God, you see, is in the detail. If you want to confess and receive God's forgiveness[3], you must tell me everything."

"Okay, Father, but remember, you promise not to tell a soul."

"I do."

Barry nods. "My name is Barry Brennan. Do you know the name?"

Another pause. "I do, my son: it's on every radio and every television. You're the prisoner[4], the one that escaped from Mountjoy prison. My son, you should let me take you to the guards[5]."

"No!" Barry shouts. "You promised, Father. No one can know."

"Then you must tell me everything."

"There's not much to tell. I escaped from the gardai van that was taking me to hospital. I told them I had a pain in my side, and the doctors thought it was my appendix[6]. When I was in the van, it stopped, and I hit one of the guards, took his keys and ran. That was two days ago."

---

1 **to promise** – *versprechen*
2 **not a soul** – *keine einzige Menschenseele*
3 **forgiveness** – *Vergebung*
4 **prisoner** – *Häftling*
5 **guard** – *garda, Polizist(in)*
6 **appendix** – *Blinddarm*

"Well, God will judge[1] you for this, my son. But tell me, why did you stay in the city? Why not run for the countryside? Or hop[2] on a ferry out of here?"

"Well, Father, there's... there's something I need to get before I can go. And that's why I'm here. I need to wait for a few days until they think I'm miles from the city. Then I can get this... thing... and I can go. And I promise, Father, after this I will never commit another crime[3] again. I will lead a quiet and honest[4] life." And Barry imagines the beaches of the Bahamas.

"I see," says the voice. "I want to help you, and if you confess[5] all your sins to me, then maybe I can. But, like I say, God is in the detail. What is this thing you need?"

Barry hesitates[6]. He thinks about lying, but why? The priest promises not to tell a soul. "It's a suitcase, Father. And inside there is half a million euros. And yes, it is stolen, but I promise, Father, no one needs it now. I stole it more than eight years ago, from a bank security van. A bank, Father, and they have insurance and all that, so they don't need it. No one needs it now apart from me."

And this time the silence is heavy and tense, and Barry can hear the voices of the women as they leave the church. He wonders[7] if there are still any people there, but he thinks there are not.

"Well..." says the quiet voice, "I understand, my son. And I will help you. I can let you sleep here for a few days, and I can bring you some food."

"Oh Father, thank you Father."

"But, like I say, God is in the detail. Where exactly is this suitcase?"

"What? Why?"

---

1   **to judge** – *beurteilen*
2   **to hop** – *springen*
3   **to commit a crime** – *ein Verbrechen begehen*
4   **honest (2)** – *aufrichtig*
5   **to confess** – *beichten*
6   **to hesitate** – *zögern*
7   **to wonder** – *sich fragen*

"Why? Because I need to know that you aren't going to hurt anyone to get it," the voice says seriously.

Barry laughs, "Oh no, Father, I promise. It's in an old garage of my brother's. On a bit of land next to Howth Road. I can go at night, dig up[1] the concrete[2] and get it, no problem."

"Well, I tell you what. You wait here. I'm going to go close the church, then maybe I can find you that bit of food and some other clothes."

And for the first time in two days, Barry Brennan feels relief[3]. He can really taste the freedom now. "Ah, thank you, Father. Thank you! You know, I'm sure there's a bit of spare money[4] for the church. Three thousand maybe? What do you think?"

But there is no answer.

There is, however, a strange noise. Something moving against the door of the confessional. Something heavy. Something like one of the heavy pews. And Barry tries to push the door open.

But he cannot.

And before Barry Brennan begins to shout and scream to the empty church, he hears the soft voice one more time.

"Now, son, I told you that any man can listen, didn't I?" it says. "And I also told you that God is in the detail. And an important detail, a very important detail, is that you're in the wrong side of the confessional. I just stopped in to confess about stealing another bottle of whiskey from the shop. But you know, I think I can do that next time. Yes, I think I might have a lot more to confess tomorrow. Now, you did say Howth Road?"

And then there is only the sound of Barry Brennan's shouts.

And there is no one in the church to hear those.

Well, apart from God, I suppose.

---

1   **to dig up** – *ausgraben*
2   **concrete** – *Beton*
3   **relief** – *Erleichterung*
4   **spare money** – *erübrigtes Geld*

Dublin ist für seine großen Grünflächen und Parkanlangen bekannt, die an das Grün der irischen Flagge erinnern. Ein sehr bedeutender und großflächiger Park Dublins ist St. Stephen's Green. Dieser Park besteht seit dem Jahre 1663, obwohl sich seine Verwendungszwecke über die Jahre stark verändert haben. Im 18. Jahrhundert fanden hier beispielsweise Hinrichtungen durch Erhängen statt. Heute werden an Sommerwochenenden kostenfreie Konzerte und Theateraufführungen angeboten.

Das Mountjoy Prison, kurz The Joy, ist ein Gefängnis für männliche Gefangene ab 17 Jahren im Norden Dublins und wurde 1850 als Mountjoy Gaol eröffnet. Hier können bis zu 540 Häftlinge untergebracht werden, obwohl es in den letzten Jahren schon vorkam, dass bis zu 670 dort inhaftiert waren.

11. ROUTE 66

The car is big and old, but it is a classic, and it moves along the road like a shark[1], the evening sun reflecting off the red paint[2].

The roof is down, and Dan enjoys the feeling of the wind in his hair. It cools him and helps him to stay awake[3]. He is tired, very tired, and he still feels sick from the beer and whiskey of last night.

Soon he can stop, find a quiet area off the road and push back the chair and sleep. But not yet: the Mojave Desert is still all around him with its flat orange sands and dead bushes. The plan was to get to Flagstaff, but it is too many miles away. So instead he just wants to get as far from the town called Needles as he can before the night comes.

Needles. He hates that town.

And that girl.

He looks at his right hand on the steering wheel[4]. The skin is raw[5], and he tries to remember exactly what happened last night, but he cannot. And maybe he should not.

Stupid girl.

But anyway, why think about it? Just drive; get a few more miles from the town, and from her.

He hits the button for the radio, and an old song fills the silence of the desert. A good song, he thinks; a real song. All guitars and rock and roll. He feels a little better. Maybe it is time for the first drink of the day after all, and he takes the small

1   **shark –** *Hai*
2   **paint –** *Lack*
3   **to stay awake –** *munter bleiben*
4   **steering wheel –** *Lenkrad*
5   **raw –** *wund*

flask[1] from the pocket of his denim jacket, removes the lid and swallows[2].

For a second the taste is foul[3]. A horrible reminder of last night, of the girl and of the hotel room. But then the hot whiskey starts to fill him, and he smiles, puts his head back and laughs loudly into the desert.

"Route Sixty-Six!" he shouts, and he turns the volume of the radio up. He can forget about last night, about the girl. His shirt has a little blood on it, and his hand is sore[4]. But he can get a new shirt, and the whiskey will help the pain.

No, this is his holiday, his escape from all those idiots back in California. Forget Needles and forget the girl. Just relax and enjoy it. She was not the first girl, and he knows she will not be the last.

Maybe there is one waiting for him in Flagstaff. And this one, he hopes, will have a little more respect for him and won't laugh at him.

So he drives, and for a while he feels better. The sun is lower in the sky now, it's a little less hot, and the radio keeps him company with old songs about love and women, rock and roll and country music. Real music.

But then the songs stop, and the news report starts. There's something about Needles, something about trouble on Route Sixty-Six, and he tries to listen, but the signal is weak[5].

"… a young… dead… the police are looking… a man, probably alone, and thought to be extremely dangerous… any information call…" and then the signal fails, and there is only the sound of the old classic engine and the silence of the desert.

"Dead? No, no it can't be her!"

ROUTE 66

He looks at his hand again and tries to make a fist[1], but it hurts.

And he thinks of the white shirt in the trunk[2] of the car: the white shirt with blood on it.

What did he do last night? He tries to remember, he tries to remember exactly what happened. He remembers the bar clearly. He remembers buying her a drink and then another and another. He remembers that afterwards they were in the hotel room kissing, but then something happened, and she laughed. She laughed at him[3], but he cannot remember why. It was something stupid: something he said or did.

And then…

But the rest is impossible to remember. He woke up late in the hotel room and was alone. He saw the blood, but there was only a little, and his hand hurt. And he knew.

Yeah, he could not remember, but he knew.

And he thinks of all the times he watched his father hit his mother.

"Jesus!" he says, and he does not feel tired anymore. He puts his foot on the accelerator[4], and the car starts to speed along the old road. Forget sleeping, forget Flagstaff. He needs to find another route and a motel to stay in for a few days: a cheap motel where they only want a name and some cash.

The sun is almost down now, the sky a deep orange and red. And the road is empty.

Or it is until he speeds past the large billboard[5]. Then suddenly the road is not empty: there is a car behind him. Its red and blue lights fill the evening, and the sound of the siren fills his ears.

---

1   **to make a fist –** *eine Faust machen*
2   **trunk –** *(AE) Kofferraum*
3   **to laugh at sb. –** *jdn. auslachen*
4   **accelerator –** *Gaspedal*
5   **billboard –** *Reklametafel*

"No!" he groans[1] as he sees it in the mirror. And he thinks for a moment about not stopping, but there is nowhere for him to go. "Jesus, just stay cool[2], Dan, just stay cool," he tries to tell himself as the red car slows down. So he stops on the edge[3] of the desert, hides the flask of whiskey under the seat and lights a cigarette to cover the smell.

God, he wishes he could remember last night: not just the girl's expression[4] when he hit her, but everything.

In the mirror he sees the cop[5] car park behind him, and he watches a young, tall cop get out.

Just one. Good. If things get serious, then maybe he can manage if there is just one.

He watches the cop walk slowly to the car. The guy's eyes are covered by silver sunglasses, and there is something strange about his uniform, Dan thinks. But before he can decide what, the cop is at the door, and Dan drops his cigarette.

"Evening, officer," he says, and tries to look sorry. "I know I was going a little too fast. I'm sorry."

The cop looks at him and nods, but says nothing. Dan wants to see the eyes behind the glasses but cannot.

"I suppose it's this road: the desert makes it easy to forget to watch your speed," he says, and he thinks he sees the cop look at his hand.

Jesus, is this it? Did he really do something to that girl? More than hit her once? Did he do what they said on the radio? Was she dead?

"Yep," the cop says, "these roads are funny like that. Lots of people have problems out here. This is a nice car. A classic. Yours?" And his voice is slow.

ROUTE 66

---

1 **to groan** – *stöhnen*
2 **to stay cool** – *ruhig bleiben*
3 **edge** – *Rand*
4 **expression** – *Gesichtsausdruck*
5 **cop** – *(AE, ugs.) Bulle*

"Yes, sir. I have my licence[1] here and the registration[2]."

The cop nods but does not take them. "I need to ask you to get out of the car."

Dan tries to smile. "Is there a problem, officer?" And he looks at the gun on the cop's belt. If he can get the gun, then he can escape. Forget California. Go north, to Canada, or Alaska.

But he waits. Maybe this is something else, a routine check[3], a formality. Be cool, Dan, he tells himself.

"Just get out of the car please," the cop repeats.

Dan nods and gets out, and he thinks again that there is something strange about the cop's uniform. It's small, too small for a tall man like him.

"I need to see in the trunk of the car, sir."

Jesus, the shirt, the shirt is in the trunk. Is that what he wants? "The trunk? Can I ask why?"

"Just routine."

Just routine? Maybe it is, and the shirt is in his bag, at the bottom where it cannot be seen. "Okay."

He walks around to the trunk, the cop behind him, and he pushes the button. For a moment he does nothing. He remembers the baseball bat[4] he keeps in there. If the cop asks to look in his bag, he can reach in, grab[5] the bat and take a swing[6]...

Maybe it can work.

"Sir?" the cop says.

"Sure," and Dan starts to lift the lid of the trunk. But in the reflection of the red paint he sees the cop raise his hand, and in the soft evening light he sees the knife, and for a moment he does not understand.

---

1   **licence** – *Führerschein*
2   **registration** – *Kraftfahrzeugbrief*
3   **routine check** – *Routinekontrolle*
4   **baseball bat** – *Baseballschläger*
5   **to grab** – *sich etw. schnappen*
6   **to take a swing** – *nach jdm. schlagen*

But then he moves. He is almost quick enough, but the knife still cuts him, and he screams and falls to the floor. The cop falls too, and there is a moment of confusion, but then Dan pushes himself up onto his feet and runs. He sees the cop car and runs to it and pulls open the door.

That's when he sees the bodies[1]. One is clearly a policewoman, but the other, a short man, has no uniform.

"Jesus!" he screams, and he remembers the news story on the radio.

"A young... dead... the police are looking... a man, probably alone, and thought to be extremely[2] dangerous... any information call..."

And he starts to run again, not on the road now, but into the desert. He wants to turn to look back to see if the man is following him, but he does not dare[3]. He thinks that if he keeps running he can escape and find help; find the real police.

But the sun is gone now, and darkness is all around him. Now everything from last night is coming back to him. He remembers hitting the girl, he remembers her shouting at him and he remembers telling her to get out.

And he remembers the last thing she said before she closed the door to the hotel room.

"I hope you die and rot[4] in the desert!" she shouted, blood still on her face.

And he almost laughs in disbelief[5].

But then he hears someone running behind him, and he screams instead.

ROUTE 66

1 **body** – *Leiche*
2 **extremely** – *äußerst*
3 **to dare** – *wagen*
4 **to rot** – *verfaulen*
5 **in disbelief** – *ungläubig*

➤ Die **Route 66**, die sich von Chicago (Illinois) bis nach Santa Monica (Kalifornien) quer durch Amerika über 3.939 Kilometer zieht, ist eine der berühmtesten Straßen der Welt und das Traumziel vieler Motorradfahrer. Die Strecke zwischen Needles (Kalifornien) und Flagstaff (Arizona), die durch die staubige Wüste führt, ist sehr einsam und hat dadurch nicht nur etwas Romantisches, sondern auch etwas Gefährliches an sich.

Als einspurige und in vielen Strecken kurvenreiche Landstraße konnte die Route 66 schon in den 1950er Jahren nicht mehr Schritt mit dem modernen wachsenden Straßenverkehr halten. Ihr wurden immer öfter die Fernstraßen vorgezogen, die in jenen Jahren massiv ausgebaut wurden.

12. THE FALL

Brandon tries not to think as he walks through the snow that reaches up[1] to his waist[2].

He is confused and weak[3].

He tries not to remember the expression on Greg's face as the bullet hit him in the back.

"You said it was easy!" Brandon calls out into the forest of silent trees that surround[4] him, his voice full of emotion. "You said no one could get hurt[5]!"

But someone did get hurt.

And now Brandon is alone, and he feels tired and lost, and he knows that the man in the dark winter coat and black hat is near. And he thinks that the next bullet is for him.

He tries to move faster through the snow, but it is so deep… and it is so cold. His clothes are wet and his skin frozen. He wants to put his hand in his coat pocket, but he has to keep the grey pistol ready.

He remembers the way that Greg fell. One moment they were running; the next there was the sound of the gun and a scream. Then Greg was on the floor; Brandon wanted to stop and help him, but Greg told him to run. To escape[6] and to not say anything to anyone. And then Brandon heard another gunshot, so he ran and left his brother in the snow to die alone.

---

1 **to reach up to –** *bis… hinaufreichen*
2 **waist –** *Taille*
3 **weak –** *schwach*
4 **to surround –** *umgeben*
5 **to get hurt –** *verletzt werden*
6 **to escape –** *fliehen*

"You said it was easy!" he shouts again and recalls[1] the first time his brother had told him about the plan.

"Listen to me," his brother said at a dark table in the corner at the Lake Louise Inn. "It's easy, Bran. I know exactly what to do."

Brandon put his beer down. "But a kid? Greg, I don't want to hurt[2] a kid."

"What?" his brother said, his eyes full of anger: "You think I do? Idiot, we won't hurt anyone. We just take the kid in the truck. Then we phone the hotel. We tell them to tell the parents they can have the kid when they leave us the money. It's easy. No one can get hurt."

But Brandon was not so sure. He knew his brother was a criminal. He knew that he brewed[3] illegal beer to sell and that he drove drugs across Alberta and British Colombia. But Brandon did not do that. He did not do any of that. He worked in the lumber yard[4], and he tried to do things right. He tried to be better than that.

But now…

"Brandon," his brother said, "I know you need the money. You don't have a job. Your truck is in pieces. You can't find work if you can't drive. What does Sally say?"

Brandon shook his head. "Sally left[5] me last month," he said, and he called the waiter for another beer. "Tell me again. Tell me everything again."

Now, alone in the forest, he thinks he can hear the sound of feet in the snow behind him, and he tries to move faster.

There is another sound too. A sound that he recognises; a sound that is getting nearer. It is like constant thunder[6] in

1   **to recall sth. –** *sich an etw. erinnern*
2   **to hurt sb. –** *jdm. wehtun*
3   **to brew –** *brauen*
4   **lumber yard –** *Holzlager*
5   **to leave –** *verlassen*
6   **thunder –** *Donner*

the distance. And he pushes through the snow, and he thinks that maybe, if he can get to the sound, he can flee[1] into the mountains and never come back.

"Look. Every year" Greg said, "hundreds of tourists come here, right? Most of them are rich, and some of them are very rich. They want to ski in the spring, hike[2] in the summer and spend their money in the hotel bar and the spa. Some of these people are millionaires, Brandon, millionaires. Think about that." Greg drank some more of his beer and looked around the bar. "Look at them. Their clothes are better than ours, their cars and trucks are better. Everything they have is better. And listen, I don't hate[3] them for that. I don't. I just know that if we ask them for a small amount[4], then they can pay. I mean twenty thousand. No more. If you ask for more, you have to wait, and then there is the risk that they contact the police. They can get twenty thousand from the bank at Banff. We tell them they only have six hours. We tell them to leave the money where we say or…"

"Or what, Greg? Or what?"

On that first day Brandon said no to the plan. On the second day he said no again. On the third day his truck stopped on the highway[5]. He had about three hundred bucks[6] left in the world. Sally was gone. Their cabin[7] by the lake was cold and empty, and there were no jobs for him anywhere.

So, on the fourth day he said yes.

The sound is louder now. Yes, it is a sound he knows. A sound he knows well. He can see nothing because of the trees, but he knows he is very near. He feels warmer now, and this

---

1 **to flee** – *flüchten*
2 **to hike** – *wandern*
3 **to hate** – *hassen*
4 **amount** – *Summe*
5 **highway** – *Schnellstraße*
6 **buck** – *(AE) Dollar*
7 **cabin** – *Hütte*

scares him. In Canada, in the mountains, when you are cold you are okay, but when you are warm, you are in trouble.

What time is it now? He does not know. He only knows that it was three in the afternoon when they first heard the sound of the police sirens.

"We have to go!" Brandon shouted. "How? How can they know where we are?" said Greg. Brandon pulled him from the old deserted[1] cabin, and they ran for Greg's truck. The sound of the sirens was still in the distance, and Brandon thought that maybe they were still okay and that maybe they could leave; maybe they could escape together.

But then there was that gunshot…

And the man in the dark winter coat and black hat, who appeared from behind the trees.

So Brandon ran. And he got to the truck and managed[2] to drive to the road, where for a few minutes he thought he was free. But then another truck appeared on the road behind him.

"But which kid?" Brandon asked as they planned everything in Greg's cabin.

"There's a family who comes here, maybe three or four times a year. The wife is a pretty little thing with red hair. I think she has family here, or maybe she comes from the area. I don't know. The husband is rich, very rich. An American. The kid looks about eleven, and they let him walk into the town from the hotel sometimes. So we watch, and we wait. When he's alone, we take him. I phone the hotel. Six hours, that's it. That's enough time for them to get the money from Banff but not enough to do anything else like phone the cops. It's easy."

So that's what they did: they took the kid as he walked into town. There was no one on the snowy road. No one saw them,

---

1   **deserted** - *verlassen*
2   **to manage to do sth.** - *es schaffen, etw. zu tun*

but they covered Greg's plates[1] to be sure, and they wore[2] masks. The kid screamed at first, but they gagged[3] him and tied his hands. Greg made the call to the hotel, and they drove to the cabin in the Yoho national park. Then they waited. Six hours to leave them the money in a safe place. No police, or the kid dies. That is what Greg told the hotel, even if that part was not true.

So how did it all go wrong[4]?

There are fewer trees now, and the sound is louder, much louder. Like the shouting of a giant.

The Takakkaw waterfalls[5]. Brandon watches the clear water tumble[6] onto the rocks, through the snow and down to the frozen forest below.

Why here?

He doesn't know. He tried to escape from the truck that chased[7] him, but he crashed on the highway. The next thing he knew he was holding his shoulder and walking confused and weak.

The falls: so beautiful, just like when he and Greg were kids. He wants to sit down to look at them and moves closer to the edge.

But no. He cannot sit down. He is sure that the man with the gun is near.

So instead he stands on the edge. He feels warm and weak, and his shoulder hurts. And he can't remember where Greg is.

"You said it was easy," he says.

"But it wasn't," a voice replies[8], and Brandon turns and sees the dark coat, only this time there is no black hat: just long, red hair. And a rifle.

1	plates –	Nummernschild
2	to wear –	tragen
3	to gag –	knebeln
4	to go wrong –	schiefgehen
5	waterfalls –	Wasserfälle
6	to tumble –	fallen
7	to chase –	verfolgen
8	to reply –	antworten

"How? How did you find us? You only had a few hours to get the money."

"My husband went for the money," says the woman, rifle in one hand, black hat in the other. "But I went to the road where you took my son. I saw the tracks[1] from your truck, and I told the police, but I made sure I found the cabin first. I know these mountains better than they do and better than you."

"I'm sorry," Brandon says, "I really am sorry. The boy is okay. He's in the back room of the cabin."

"I know," the woman says.

"Are you going to shoot[2] me?" he asks.

There is only the sound of the waterfall for a moment. Then the woman turns and moves back into the trees. He feels his legs shake and falls down onto the red and white snow by the waterfall.

"*I already did*" she calls back to him as she slowly disappears from sight.

---

1   **track** – *Spur*
2   **to shoot sb.** – *jdn. erschießen*

Der **Takakkaw Wasserfall** befindet sich im Yoho Nationalpark in British Columbia. Mit seinen 254 Metern zählt er zu den höchsten Wasserfällen Kanadas. Der Wasserfall entspringt dem Daly Gletscher.

Die Region ist außergewöhnlich schön und nicht nur dank ihrer Unberührtheit ein beliebtes Ziel für Touristen und Naturliebhaber. Hier kann man Fahrradtouren machen, wandern, klettern, zelten und angeln. Im Winter kann man außerdem Skilanglaufen und Schneeschuhwandern. Im Yoho Nationalpark befindet sich zudem der Burgess-Schiefer, eine 505 Millionen Jahre alte Fossillagerstätte.

THE FALL

13. THE OLD SCHOOL TIE

The police car stops in the driveway[1] of the school, and the two detectives get out and look around. Detective Smith is older, his hair a mixture of black and grey, his stomach[2] large, and his expression usually unhappy. The other detective, West, is younger and thinner but with an empty look in his eye.

"Look at this place," says Smith.

In the distance the church towers, cathedral and university buildings of the city of Oxford are all visible[3]. Around the old but impressive[4] school, there are green gardens and grounds[5] that continue for miles, and at the windows of the building there are the thirty faces of serious young men, who watch them strangely[6].

"God, what kind of kid goes to a school like this?"

West nods but does not say anything. After only two weeks of working with Smith, he already knows that it is best to just nod.

"Come on," Smith says, and they walk to the entrance.

Inside, the school smells of wood and polish[7], and on the walls there are antique pictures of old teachers and respected students.

"Not like my school."

"Sir[8]?"

"I went to a real[9] school. A comprehensive[10]. You?"

1	**driveway –** *Auffahrt*
2	**stomach –** *Bauch*
3	**visible –** *sichtbar*
4	**impressive –** *imposant*
5	**grounds –** *Anlagen*
6	**strangely –** *seltsam*
7	**polish –** *Politur*
8	**Sir? –** *Wie, bitte?*
9	**real –** *echt*
10	**comprehensive school** ≈ *Gesamtschule*

"Er, a grammar school[1], Sir." And Smith nods his head and says nothing.

The secretary outside the headmaster's[2] room tells them they can enter, but Smith stops. "Listen, West. I do the talking, you make the notes[3]. The best thing a good detective can do is listen and observe[4]. Write that down."

"Yes, Sir."

The headmaster is a man about the same age as Smith, but there the comparison[5] ends. Smith looks tired, old and unhappy. The headmaster, Mr Bowen, does not exactly look happy, but he looks content[6]. Content with his job, his life, his expensive house and his two expensive cars.

Smith hates him instantly.

The secretary, a young and pretty blonde, enters the room and sits by the table. The headmaster tells them to sit in the same voice he uses for his students.

"Miss White is here to take notes and can give you some more details about Mr Fletcher."

"Mr Fletcher?" asks Smith.

"Yes." Bowen stands by the large windows and does not look at them. "He's why you're here. Don't you know that?"

"No. The chief inspector[7] told us to come, but he didn't say why."

"Ah, yes, James. We play golf together. Good man. Well, the problem is that we can't find one of our members of staff: Mr Fletcher."

"A missing person[8]. I see. When did you last see him?"

"Miss White?

1	**grammar school** ≈ *Gymnasium*
2	**headmaster** – *Schulleiter*
3	**to make notes** – *Notizen machen*
4	**to observe** – *beaobachten*
5	**comparison** – *Vergleich*
6	**content** – *zufrieden*
7	**chief inspector** – *Hauptkommissar*
8	**missing person** – *vermisste Person*

"His last class was yesterday at four. He was teaching the upper sixth form[1] boys. Geometry. They say he finished class[2] at five and left as normal."

"I see. Then he went home?"

"Mr Fletcher lives on the grounds of the school. Several of the older teachers do. He lives alone on the second floor in the east wing. Two other teachers live there, but neither saw him."

Smith is about to speak when a loud hammering sound starts, and Bowen shakes his head. "Sorry about that. Building work[3]. Several areas in the school are being renovated."

Smith speaks up[4]. "And did he leave the school last night?"

"We don't know. He normally doesn't. He takes his meals in the room. But last night he didn't call for anything."

"Is that strange?"

"Not uncommon[5]. Sometimes he prefers to have a sherry and a cigar and nothing more. But when he didn't come to breakfast this morning, we began to worry[6]."

Smith looks at the clock. "Mr Bowen, normally we need to wait forty-eight hours until we can start a missing-person investigation."

Bowen turns from the window and gives Smith an annoyed[7] look. "Your chief inspector said you could help. Was he wrong?"

Smith sighs[8] and shakes his head. "Does Mr Fletcher have any good friends here? Or more importantly, enemies[9]?"

"He is a solitary[10] man. But respected. He is the oldest teacher at Barnaby's: practically part of the building." Bowen stops and

---

1   **upper sixth form** ≈ *gymnasiale Oberstufe*
2   **class** – *Unterricht*
3   **building work** – *Bauarbeiten*
4   **to speak up** – *lauter sprechen*
5   **uncommon** – *ungewöhnlich*
6   **to worry** – *sich Sorgen machen*
7   **annoyed** – *verärgert*
8   **to sigh** – *seufzen*
9   **enemy** – *Feind*
10   **solitary** – *einsam*

thinks. "He doesn't like our new music teacher, Mr Cliff. Didn't they have some sort of fight recently, Miss White?"

"I don't think so," she says quietly.

"And what about the students?" Smith asks them both.

"The students?" replies Bowen in an insulted[1] tone. "Detective, the young men at this school are very clever and come from very important families. In a few years they will be politicians, judges or doctors. They are not criminals."

Smith breathes out with a puff[2]. "No. Well, I suppose[3] we could have a look around the school…"

"Good," says Bowen. "Show them out[4] Miss White." And the headmaster does not look at them again.

"Jesus," says Smith in the corridor. "Who does he think he is? Just because he plays golf with the chief inspector. Waste of bloody time[5] this is, West. Did you hear him? This Fletcher likes a sherry. He's drunk somewhere; that's all this is. In some pub in the city."

And West nods again.

They walk along the corridors for five minutes and reach an internal courtyard[6]. Outside they can see the renovation work: there is scaffolding[7] on the face of the old building, a new wall on the side of it, and three or four workmen[8] are sitting on a bench eating lunch.

They cross the courtyard, and Smith stops to pick up a school tie[9] on the floor by the new wall. "Politicians and doctors? They can't even dress themselves." And Smith puts the tie in his pocket.

1	**insulted** – *beleidigt*	
2	**puff** – *Atemstoß*	
3	**to suppose** – *vermuten*	
4	**to show sb. out** – *jdn. hinausbegleiten*	
5	**waste of time** – *Zeitverschwendung*	
6	**courtyard** – *Innenhof*	
7	**scaffolding** – *Baugerüst*	
8	**workman** – *Handwerker*	
9	**school tie** – *Krawatte der Schuluniform*	

"Sir, look!" West says and points to the top of a tower.

"What?"

"There were two people watching us, Sir."

"And?"

"Well, just observing, Sir. Maybe there's a connection."

Smith sighs. "I do the thinking," he says. "Okay, one look, and then we go. We can also check one or two of the local pubs on the way back to the city."

The door to the tower is in another corridor, and when they open it, they hear footsteps[1] on the stairs. "Who's that?" Smith shouts.

The footsteps stop, and Miss White steps into view.

"You? Were you watching us from the roof?"

"No, well, not really," the secretary says quietly.

"Who else is with you…? Mr Fletcher?"

"What? No!"

"Be honest now, or there might be trouble[2] for you."

"It's my fault[3]," a voice says, and a young man steps forward. "Miss White came to speak to me."

"Oh really, and who are you?"

"I'm the music teacher, Mr Cliff."

"Ah, well. Isn't that interesting?"

"No, it's not what you think. I came here to tell Mr Cliff what the headmaster said about the argument."

"Go on."

"Look," says Cliff, "it was nothing, really. Only, Fletcher said something about Miss White: something no gentleman should say. I told him to apologise[4], and then we argued. But the last time I saw him was yesterday morning."

"It's true," adds[5] Miss White.

---

1 **footstep –** *Schritt*
2 **trouble –** *Ärger*
3 **fault –** *Schuld*
4 **to apologise –** *um Entschuldigung bitten*
5 **to add –** *hinzufügen*

"Well, we might need to talk to you again at another time," Smith says and turns to go back to the courtyard. But then he stops. "How did you know Mr Cliff was here, Miss White?"

The secretary blushes[1]. "We… meet here… sometimes… for lunch."

"Ah, I see."

Then the hammering they heard in the headmaster's office starts again, and the policemen go to the door.

"Detective," says the secretary. "You asked about the students. They hate Mr Fletcher. They say he punishes[2] them for every mistake[3]."

"Well, students normally don't like teachers, do they?"

"Fletcher is worse," says Cliff. "He's a dinosaur. I think he hits the boys sometimes, but I can't prove[4] it."

Smith nods. "I'm sure it's nothing."

Back in the courtyard Smith stops by the workmen, who are still sitting and eating their lunch. "Listen and observe, West. I suppose you didn't notice, but those two are having some sort of romantic affair."

"Er, well, yes I did notice, Sir."

"You did? Good. I can teach you a few things I think, West." And Smith nods to the workmen.

"Should we speak to the students, Sir?" West asks as they walk back to the car.

"What for?"

"Well, to see if they know anything."

Smith takes the tie from his pocket. "They're children, West: they can't even put a tie on. Let's get back to the city." And he throws the tie on the floor.

---

1   **to blush** – *erröten*
2   **to punish** – *bestrafen*
3   **mistake** – *Fehler*
4   **to prove** – *beweisen*

West nods. It's best to just nod. But there is something that does not make sense. The hammering noise. They heard it in the headmaster's office. And they heard it in the corridor with Miss White and Mr Cliff.

And he looks back at the workmen, who are enjoying a slow lunch.

But if these men are not hammering…

"Come on, West!" Smith shouts, and West nods.

Yes, it's best to just nod.

And somewhere in the dark Mr Fletcher stops hammering his foot against the new wall. He is tired now. Very tired.

He tries to remember exactly what happened. He remembers hitting that idiot of a boy Harris because he made a mistake in the geometry class. He remembers another boy telling him to stop. Then another boy. And another. And then they were all on top of him[1]. At first they only hit him. But then he felt school ties being wrapped[2] around his hands and feet and mouth. And they lifted him up and carried him to the new wall, which was nearly finished. And they put him behind it, in a deep dark corner where no one could see him and the light disappeared as they put the last bricks[3] in place. He tried desperately to shout, but he could not, and he tried to move, but he could not. And for a while he thought that he would die in the deep dark corner behind the wall.

But everything will be okay now, he knows. Because after hours of struggling his foot is now finally free to move.

And the police will be here soon, he is sure.

And they will hear.

So he continues to hammer his foot against the wall.

And he hopes that someone hears him soon.

---

1 **they were all on top of him** – *sie fielen alle über ihn her*
2 **wrap** – *umwickeln*
3 **brick** - *Baustein*

Preparatory schools, oder 'prep schools', sind Privatschulen, die sich darauf spezialisiert haben, die britischen Eliteschüler auf die Herausforderungen der Public Schools vorzubereiten. Die Schüler sind hier zwischen 8 und 13 Jahre alt. Im 19. Jahrhundert waren prep schools ausschließlich Internatsschulen.

Public Schools oder Independent Schools sind im Vereinigten Königreich Schulen, die durch Schulgebühren finanziert werden. Die ersten Public Schools waren damals dazu bestimmt, begabten Kindern die Chance einer Schulbildung zu vermitteln, unabhängig von der finanziellen Situation der Familie. Daher stammt die Bezeichnung Public School. Der größte Teil der Schüler waren normal zahlende Schüler.

14. THE POACHERS

"My God! Just look at that, Junior," Owen says with a smile, and he points[1] to the valley and green forest below them. "Abertreweren Forest. What a beauty, hey, lad[2]?" And he looks to his son, Owen Junior, and he wants to see a smile on the boy's pale[3] face, but, like always, there is nothing but[4] disinterest.

"We saw it last year," Junior says. "It just looks the same."

"The same? Well, I suppose, but look at it, Son. Look at how beautiful it is. Can there be a finer place in Wales? I don't think so."

But Junior only shrugs[5].

Owen shakes his head. He remembers when he came here with his father to poach[6] a few rabbits as a child. He loved the walk up from the town of Sennybridge; he loved the hours of walking and hunting[7] in the forests and valley.

But not Junior. Junior said that to walk there was stupid, because they had a car, and despite[8] all of Owen's arguments, the teenager did not change his mind.

Owen looks back at the car and hopes that no one can see it from the main road. He lifts the two gun bags onto his shoulder and starts to walk. "Come on, Son, this is going to be great fun," he says, and Junior follows him but says nothing.

The forest is alive with life.

1	**to point to sth.** – *auf etw. zeigen*	
2	**lad** – *(BE) Kumpel*	
3	**pale** – *blass*	
4	**nothing but** – *nichts außer*	
5	**to shrug** – *mit den Achseln zucken*	
6	**to poach** – *wildern*	
7	**to hunt** – *jagen*	
8	**despite** – *trotz*	

It is the second week of April, and spring is certainly here. The grass below their feet is green and fresh, the trees are heavy with leaves, and the air smells so good that Owen forgets about Junior's mood[1]. "Smell that, Son. Good, hey? That's the scent of life. The scent of the real Wales."

Junior lifts his head. "I can't smell anything."

"What? The flowers, the trees. Spring!"

"Oh, that." And the boy pulls something out of his pocket, and Owen sees that it is his mp3 player.

"Whoa[2] whoa whoa!" he says. "Wait a minute, Son, you don't need that today."

"What? But I want to listen to my music."

"Music? Listen to the forest, lad. Listen to the birds and the wind. No, you don't need that today," he repeats, and he takes the mp3 player from the boy's hands, and he tries to avoid the angry look in the boy's dark eyes.

Dark eyes. Just like his mother's. And dark hair too, just like his mother's.

Owen is tall and fair[3] with blue eyes and a healthy complexion[4] from years of work and activity outside.

Junior is short for his age. Short and thin with a pale and unhealthy complexion from hours of playing his computer games and watching television.

When Owen was a boy of fourteen, he played rugby or football every day, he ran to the school in the village just for fun, and he spent every Sunday in the forests with his dad.

Junior does not like sports, he does not run, and the last time he came to the forest with Owen, he said that he was too cold and that the forest was boring[5].

1   mood – *Laune*
2   Whoah! – *Langsam!*
3   to be fair – *helles Haar haben*
4   complexion – *Teint*
5   boring – *langweilig*

But Owen does not like to think about that too much. His wife Rhea is a good woman and pretty too, but sometimes he cannot help but[1] look at Junior and wonder[2].

So he tries not to think about it.

Rhea says that it is just his age, and that all teenage boys prefer computer games and television to walks in the forest.

And yes, the last time they came to the forest, it was a bit cold, and they had nothing to do.

But not this time. No, this time the sun is high and hot, and this time Owen has his old guns over his shoulder, and he remembers the way that Junior's expressionless[3] face changed when he saw them the night before.

"These were your granddad's[4] guns," he said to him in the kitchen. "And one day they can be yours if you want."

"Really? And I can shoot[5] things: animals and things?"

"Of course lad, but I need to show you how first."

"But I know how."

"You do?"

"Yeah, I saw how in films and on television."

Owen laughed. "Ha, well, I need to show you how to do it safely, so we need to go up to the old Abertreweren forest."

And Owen knew the boy was interested then, and for the first time in a long time he thought that maybe there was something they could do together. Father and son: the way it should be.

But now in the forest he is not so sure. The boy looks bored[6] already, and he is not looking at the gun bags with interest any more.

Well, maybe when he gets to shoot one.

---

1 **cannot help but** – *nicht umhin kommen, etw. zu tun*
2 **to wonder** – *sich wundern*
3 **expressionless** – *ausdruckslos*
4 **granddad** – *Opa*
5 **to shoot** – *schießen*
6 **bored** – *gelangweilt*

Soon they are deep in the forest, and Owen finds a small clearing[1]. He puts the guns next to a tree and takes them out of the bags carefully[2], and, yes, there is the interest in the boy's eyes.

"So what can we shoot?" Junior asks.

"At this time of year, we want to look for rabbits[3], Son, but if we can get a hare[4], even better."

"What about deer[5]? Can we shoot them?"

"Deer? No, Son. They're too big. We don't want to carry a deer back to the car: someone might see us."

"So?"

And Owen realises that the boy does not understand what poaching is.

"Well, you see, really, we aren't supposed to[6] be here."

"What?" Junior says, a scared look in his eyes. "Why not?"

"Well, to some people shooting here is illegal. They call it 'poaching."

"Which people?"

"Well, the police, for example. And the Forestry Commission[7]."

Junior looks around the forest. "You mean it's a crime? It's illegal?"

Owen thinks about what to say. "Well, it is, Son, but only like downloading films for free. That's a crime, that's illegal, but you still do that, don't you? Well, this is just like that. No one gets hurt. We take one or two rabbits home and we have a little fun. That's okay, isn't it?"

Junior nods. "I suppose so. But what if someone sees us?"

"Ah, good question, Son. Now, not many people come to this side of the forest at this time of the year, but if you see

---

1	**clearing** – *Waldlichtung*
2	**carefully (1)** – *vorsichtig*
3	**rabbit** – *Kaninchen*
4	**hare** – *Hase*
5	**deer** – *Reh*
6	**not to be supposed to** – *nicht dürfen*
7	**Forestry Commission** – *zuständige Behörde für Forstwirtschaft*

someone you just put the gun down gently[1] in a bush or under some leaves[2]. Remember to do it nice and gently and to say hello. If you have no gun, then there is no problem; we can come back for the gun another day. Okay? So remember: if you see or hear someone, put it down nice and gently, and there will be no problem."

Junior looks a bit happier now, and for twenty minutes Owen talks to him about how to hold the gun and how to walk with it, while his son listens carefully[3] and asks sensible questions[4] that show a real interest. For the first time in many years Owen and Junior seem to be exactly what they are: father and son. And Owen now notices that the boy actually looks a little bit like him after all and that he also smiles sometimes.

Sure, he likes films and television and not sports, but maybe this can be their thing. It doesn't have to be every weekend if Junior does not want to, but occasionally. Then maybe in a few years they can start to go for a pint[5] like Owen and his father did.

"Right then, Son," he says feeling extremely happy and enjoying the excitement in his boy's eyes. "Now, I'm going to load[6] the guns, and then we can follow the path there into the forest. Do you remember the rules about the gun, Son?"

"Yes, Dad. Keep the gun pointed down to the ground unless[7] I see a rabbit. Never point the gun at you or anyone else. Keep to your left but not directly behind you. Don't shoot unless I can clearly see that there is no one near the target. And don't forget there are two shots[8] and that I should empty[9] the gun before I give it back to you."

"Exactly!" says Owen, and he feels full of pride[1] and thinks what a wonderful day this is: out in the beauty of the Welsh countryside with his son.

And for a while they walk, and he is happy about how carefully Junior holds the gun and how he listens and does exactly what he should. But then they reach[2] another clearing, and they hear something behind the trees.

"Dad?" Junior whispers, and he looks scared "what's that noise? Is it the police?"

And Owen signals him to be quiet[3]. He tries to see through the trees but he cannot. He thinks there is someone or something moving, and it is big: bigger than a rabbit or a hare, but he does not think it can be a person. He never sees people up here at this time of year. In the summer maybe, but not now.

Could it be a park ranger[4] from the Forestry Commission? Did someone see the car parked in the trees and call the police?

There is a snap from behind the trees, and Owen thinks that maybe he should put his gun down, in a bush, nice and carefully like he told Junior to do. Behind him he can hear Junior, who sounds like he is very scared.

But then Owen sees what is behind the trees: brown hair, big gentle eyes… He laughs and turns back to Junior to tell him to stay calm.

But before he can do this, Junior, who does not know what is making the noise, remembers his dad's words:

"… if you have no gun, then there is no problem…"

But he does not remember the other words…

… put it down gently…

Owen sees the boy throw the gun and tries to shout that it is just a deer, but it is too late. There is a loud bang[5]. Owen feels

---

1 **pride –** *Stolz*
2 **to reach –** *erreichen*
3 **quiet –** *still*
4 **park ranger –** *Parkaufseher*
5 **bang –** *Knall*

an incredible pain in his behind[1], and he screams and falls to the floor.

As he lies there shouting and screaming and trying to pull the pieces of shot[2] from his skin, he looks up at the beautiful blue sky and green trees and magnificent[3] forest.

And he thinks that maybe next time they should just go to the cinema instead. Or maybe play a computer game or watch television.

---

1 **behind –** *Hintern*
2 **shot –** *Schrot*
3 **magnificent –** *grandios*

Die Landschaften von **Wales** sind vermutlich die schönsten und unberührtesten Landstriche Großbritanniens und Irlands: Abertreweren ist nur einer von Hunderten von Wäldern im Brecon Beacons National-park.

Im angelsächsischen England war es allen erlaubt – nicht nur den Königen und Adligen – die Natur für den Eigenbedarf zu nutzen. Mit der normannischen Invasion im Jahre 1066 hielt auch das feudalistische System des kontinentalen Europa auf den Inseln Einzug. Dieses neue System untersagte es nicht nur, in den Wäldern zu jagen, sondern verbot darüber hinaus das Fällen von Bäumen oder das Sammeln von bereits gefälltem Holz, sowie von Beeren oder anderen Früchten.

15. THE CARD SHARK

"Are you sitting comfortably? Good.

I want to tell you a little story that I know. Now, it's not a very nice story, and I can't promise you that there will be a very happy ending. But it's a true story, and that's something that's very important to me, and I want you to remember that.

Yeah, you need to remember that the truth is important to me. And you know what? It's something that's very important to you too.

Or it should be.

So relax a little, and listen.

See, there was once a young man called Jimmy Lane. An Englishman from the great city of London. Well, Jimmy was a nobody in many ways. You know what I mean when I say a nobody? I mean Jimmy wasn't rich, and he wasn't too bright[1], you know? Not very clever, really. And he wasn't a funny guy, and he didn't have much luck with the ladies. I know all this to be true. I know it because I can read people, and I could see all this when I looked at Jimmy Lane.

However, Jimmy had a talent. A skill. An ability.

You see, Jimmy could play cards.

Poker, blackjack, rummy: you name the game and Jimmy could play it, though he especially liked poker. With a deck of cards[2] in his hands, Jimmy was like a magician[3]. He could cut and shuffle[4] the deck like he had eight arms instead of two, and

---

1   **bright** – *intelligent*
2   **deck of cards** – *Kartenset*
3   **magician** – *Zauberer*
4   **to shuffle** – *mischen*

he could remember every card he saw in a split second[1] and could use his fingers and little tricks to put the cards where he wanted them in the deck.

Oh boy[2], what a talent! What a skill Jimmy had!

And he had something else too.

He had a choice. A choice about what to do with this talent. You see, there are two things you can do with a talent like that. You can either[3] play the game right: you play it straight[4]. This way you enter the competitions, you play your best, and you play by the rules. Then slowly you win respect, and slowly you make a name for yourself.

Or[3] there's the other thing you can do.

You can cheat[5].

Do you know what I mean when I say cheat? I mean you use the little tricks, the fast fingers and the good memory, but you use it to break the rules of the game.

And do you know what choice Jimmy Lane made?

You got it[6].

He decided to cheat. He decided to come to the biggest, richest, most important gambling city[7] in the world, and he decided to cheat.

That's right. He couldn't wait[8]. He wanted everything now. He wanted money, he wanted to be famous, and he wanted respect.

So yeah, he came here. To Las Vegas.

Vegas, wow! What a city! The lights, the music, the atmosphere.

And Jimmy thought he could take it all.

THE CARD SHARK

---

1   **in a split second** - *im Bruchteil einer Sekunde*
2   **Oh boy!** - *Junge, Junge!*
3   **either... or** - *entweder... oder*
4   **to play it straight** - *ehrlich sein*
5   **to cheat** - *schummeln*
6   **You got it.** - *Genau!*
7   **gambling city** - *Glücksspielstadt*
8   **He couldn't wait.** - *Er konnte es kaum erwarten.*

Ha! What a kid. What a dumb[1], stupid kid.

You see, you don't take from Las Vegas: Vegas takes from you.

But Jimmy, poor, stupid Jimmy, didn't know that. So he found a casino. A real casino, one of the best in the city. And he thought he could do it quickly. Play the game, get the money and run before anyone knew he was there.

But he picked[2] the wrong casino.

He picked my casino.

That was a bad decision. But worse than that was his next decision. That was when he decided he was good enough and clever enough and lucky enough to play at my table. To enter my Golden Chip competition. A competition where only the best of the best get to play. How he made the money to enter, I don't know. I think he probably cheated to get that too. But he entered my competition, and he used his tricks and his fast fingers, and he won every game until it came to the final."

Hank Wynn stops talking and puts his cigar back in his mouth. He looks calm. Happy almost. But there is something very dangerous about Hank Wynn when he looks calm and happy. Some people say that the reason his casino is called Shark Pool is because Hank looks a little like a shark. He always wears a grey suit, he always walks in a slow manner, and his eyes are always cold and dark.

But maybe there is another reason for the name of the casino.

"The truth, Jimmy." And Hank throws the end of the cigar into the pool in front of him.

It is night time, and around the roof[3] of the thirty-floor casino and hotel, the city of Las Vegas is alive with colour. There are people everywhere, but here on the roof there are only four people. There is Hank Wynn and his assistants and bodyguards,

---

1   **dumb** – *(AE) dumm*
2   **to pick** – *auswählen*
3   **roof** – *Dach*

Kenny and Clive, who stand patiently[1] and listen to his speech. And there is Jimmy Lane.

Jimmy Lane does not stand. Jimmy Lane cannot stand.

His hands are tied[2]. His legs are tied. And his mouth is gagged[3].

And there is blood on Jimmy Lane. Small cuts on his arms and chest, and he is naked apart from his trousers.

"Now, I am a not a cruel man, Jimmy. I'm really not. I'm a business man, not a gangster. But this city is cruel, Jimmy. And sometimes I have to do things to protect my business. Do you understand that, Jimmy? Do you know how many kids like you come into my casino? No? Hundreds, thousands. They all think they can win. They all think they can cheat and beat[4] the casino." And Jimmy Lane shakes his head and tries to say something, and his blue eyes are wet[5].

"Wait a moment, Jimmy. Wait one moment," Hank says, and he puts his hand on Jimmy's head, and Jimmy tries to move away. "I don't want you to say anything stupid, Jimmy, because this is your last chance." He looks across the pool to his assistant. "When did they last[6] eat, Clive?"

"Last week, Mr Wynn. You remember the Mexican: the one stealing[7] from the bar?"

"Ah, yes. A week. Did you hear that, Jimmy? So before I take this gag out of your mouth, and before you think about saying something stupid again, think about this. Did you really not think that we were watching you? We knew you were cheating. We knew you were using your little tricks. The only reason you got to the final table, to my table, Jimmy is because I let you."

1 **patiently** – *geduldig*
2 **tied** – *gebunden*
3 **gagged** – *geknebelt*
4 **to beat** – *besiegen*
5 **wet** – *feucht*
6 **last** – *zum letzten Mal*
7 **to steal** – *stehlen*

THE CARD SHARK

And Hank takes Jimmy's face in his hands. "The truth, Jimmy. I want the truth. It's very important to me. And, right now, it's very important to you." And he takes the gag from Jimmy's mouth.

For a moment Jimmy is silent. Then he shouts as loud as he can. "Help me! Somebody, we're on the roof! Help me!"

And for a moment Hank is silent. Then he laughs, and the two assistants laugh, and then the back of Hank's hand slaps[1] Jimmy's face hard. "Oh, Jimmy. You really are a stupid kid. We're miles up above one of the loudest cities in the world. No one can hear you. No one but me and the boys. So Jimmy, one last chance. Tell me, tell me the truth."

And Jimmy looks at the pool and the clear water, and he nods. "Okay, okay. You're right Mr Wynn. Everything you said about me is right. I was a nobody. I was never rich, I was never too clever. But I can play cards. I started playing when I was seven or eight, with friends at school, online, in local competitions. And I'm good. I mean, I'm really good. And yeah, that's why I came here. I wanted to win, I wanted the respect you talked about. Is that a crime[2]? Is that wrong?"

Hank slaps him again, "No, Jimmy, but cheating in my casino is!"

"I didn't cheat!" Jimmy shouts, and he is angry now. "I never cheat. You can hit me, or you can try to scare[3] me, but I never cheat!"

Hank Wynn laughs. "Scare you? You think we want to scare you? Clive, let them out," he says.

Clive nods and pushes a button on a control panel[4] next to the pool. Below the water a metal door slides open[5]. For a moment there is nothing, but then two long, grey shapes[6] appear in the clear water, and Jimmy starts to shout again.

1	**to slap** – *ohrfeigen*
2	**crime** – *Verbrechen*
3	**to scare sb.** – *jdn. erschrecken*
4	**control panel** – *Bedienungspult*
5	**to slide open** – *aufschieben*
6	**shape** – *Gestalt*

"You cheated, Jimmy. Four aces[1]? I know you put those cards in. I don't know how, but I know!"

"No, Mr Wynn! I didn't, I promise! I didn't, I don't cheat, I never cheat!"

For a moment Hank Wynn stops, and maybe there is a second where he believes poor Jimmy Lane. But then the second is over, and he kicks[2] Jimmy in the back, and Jimmy falls into the pool with a scream.

Hank Wynn does not stop to watch what happens next. He never does. You see, he is not a cruel man, but he sometimes has to do cruel things. "Come on," he says to Clive and Kenny, and they move back to the stairs.

"But, Mr Wynn, how did you know he cheated? We didn't see anything on the cameras," Clive asks.

Hank shakes his head. "Idiot! I always take the aces out of the pack and make sure that[3] I get the kings," he says, and he goes back into his casino to play another game.

But for a moment Clive and Kenny wait, stepping backwards so that the waves caused by the feeding frenzy[4] do not get at them.

For a moment Clive is silent. But then he slowly says something as if he does not himself believe what he is saying. "I… I changed the pack of cards before the last game. I never told Mr Wynn."

"You mean…?"

Clive nods. "The aces were in the pack."

And for a little while more they wait, until the surface[5] of the pool is calm again. "I guess he was telling the truth, then."

And they shut the door on what remains of Jimmy Lane.

1   **ace –** *Ass*
2   **to kick –** *treten*
3   **to make sure that –** *dafür sorgen, dass…*
4   **feeding frenzy –** *Futterstreit*
5   **surface –** *Oberfläche*

Las Vegas ist die Unterhaltungshauptstadt der Welt, oder weniger positiv ausgedrückt, die Sündenstadt. Mitten in der Wüste, ist Las Vegas berühmt für seine unzähligen Unterhaltungsmöglichkeiten für Erwachsene. Die bekannteste Form ist das Glücksspiel, das auch oft in Film und Fernsehen, Zeitschriften und Literatur gezeigt wird.

16. THE TUBE

The air of the tube[1] platform is hot and dry, and the lights weak and unnatural.

Sarah considers sitting on one of the seats by the wall of the tunnel, but she is so tired that she thinks that maybe she will fall asleep if she rests.

So she stands, and she looks around at her fellow commuters[2] and other passengers. Twenty tired faces: some talking, but most are silent and waiting like her.

She looks at the electronic clock.

It is seven thirty-six: her train should be here in two minutes.

For a moment she thinks about how quiet the platform is, and how normally she has to fight[3] to get on the train in the evening.

But there will be no fighting today: the few people that are here look half dead. Exhausted from a long day at work and made passive by the slow journey[4] home.

Home.

Sarah thinks about her cosy[5] sofa and the Chinese takeaway she will eat while watching TV. She can get it as she passes the restaurant, buy a bottle of wine from the local shop and be in bed by ten o'clock.

It is a comforting[6] but also rather depressing thought.

But that's life.

---

1   **tube** – *Londoner U-Bahn*
2   **commuter** – *Pendler*
3   **to fight** – *kämpfen*
4   **journey** – *Fahrt*
5   **cosy** – *gemütlich*
6   **comforting** – *beruhigend*

Work, eat, sleep.

She hears the train in the dark tunnel and tells herself to wake up and to focus for another forty minutes.

The forty minutes from Liverpool Street to North Acton.

The train speeds[1] out of the tunnel, and she enjoys the feeling of the wind in her dark brown hair. As it stops, she sees her reflection in the mirror of the carriage[2].

I look like death, she thinks.

The doors of the carriages open, a few people get off, and Sarah and the commuters get on.

Inside the carriage it is even hotter than on the platform, but it is almost empty too.

She finds a seat and sits down.

Do not fall asleep[3], she tells herself.

She looks around the carriage: there are only eight other people there: a young couple[4] holding hands and talking quietly on the seat opposite her; two businessmen a few seats to her right; an old lady two seats to her left; a mother and son at the far end of the carriage. And a strange-looking man in a coat in the corner.

A strange man.

Is he strange? Or are you just being silly[5]?

She looks at him. She cannot see his face because he has the hood[6] of his sports jacket up, but he seems to be asleep, and there is something about his face that she does not like. He has a short beard and pale, unhealthy skin, and she thinks that his eyes are probably unkind[7].

The train starts, and she shakes her head.

1   **to speed** – *flitzen*
2   **carriage** – *Wagen*
3   **to fall asleep** – *einschlafen*
4   **couple** – *Paar*
5   **silly** – *albern*
6   **hood** – *Kapuze*
7   **unkind** – *unfreundlich*

You are an idiot, she tells herself and pulls a book out of her bag. On the front there is a picture of a man with a short beard and pale skin and unkind eyes. She almost laughs.

You need to stop reading this rubbish[1]: you are losing your mind[2], she tells herself.

The man in the corner is probably just a normal guy and not some horrible character from one of her thrillers.

For ten minutes she reads her crime novel[3]. She starts to feel better: more relaxed and less concerned[4] about the reason why the tube is so quiet today.

Then the train stops at another station. There are loud voices on the platform and Sarah knows why.

The doors slide open, and ten or twelve students from Chancery High School enter the carriage.

The old woman two seats away from her does not look happy and she moves to sit in the seat next to Sarah.

"Do you mind[5], dear[6]?"

"No, of course not," Sarah says and smiles. The poor old woman must not feel too comfortable next to the noisy kids, but Sarah knows that they are okay: she can spot the bad kids from a mile away[7].

She is, after all, a teacher.

No, these kids are okay, but they are loud, and it is impossible for Sarah not to hear their conversation. And when she hears the topic[8] that they are talking about, she suddenly feels cold.

"Yeah, he killed another one, didn't he? Last Friday, they reckon[9]," the tallest of the kids says.

1	**rubbish** – *(BE) Müll*
2	**to lose one's mind** – *den Verstand verlieren*
3	**crime novel** – *Kriminalroman*
4	**concerned** – *besorgt*
5	**Do you mind?** – *Stört es Sie?*
6	**dear** – *Schatz (auch unter Fremden)*
7	**to spot sth. from a mile away** – *sofort erkennen*
8	**topic** – *Thema*
9	**to reckon** – *meinen*

THE TUBE

"I know, sick, isn't it? I mean, how many is that now?" asks another.

"Six?"

"No, man, seven."

"Is it? Man, you know, the sick thing is that no one knows who it is. They don't know if it's a man, a woman, some kid, you get[1] me?"

"No, the sick thing is the way he kills them. He uses something strange: not a knife but something long and thin, and he stabs[2] them again and again, and they just bleed and bleed."

"Yeah, but the weird[3] thing is none of them tried to fight," says the tall kid.

"How do you know that?"

"Coz[4] the newspapers said it. They said none of the victims looked like they tried to fight. They just, I don't know, let this guy stab them again and again."

And now there is silence in the carriage, and Sarah sees that everyone is listening to the conversation.

But she does not want to listen, and she takes her MP3 player from her bag and puts her headphones in.

She does not want to think about their conversation or the horrible reason why the tube is so quiet. She does not want to think about the stories in the newspapers.

She does not want to think about what the police are calling *the tube murders.*

She closes her eyes and thinks about her sofa, her Chinese take-away and her bed. After a few more minutes she feels the train stop and she is aware[5] of the kids getting off.

Just listen to the music, she tells herself. Relax and rest.

---

1   **to get –** *(BE, ugs.) verstehen*
2   **to stab sb. –** *jdn. niederstechen*
3   **weird –** *seltsam*
4   **coz –** *(ugs.) weil*
5   **to be aware –** *merken*

But don't sleep.

Don't…

But she is exhausted[1], and her head begins to drop, and she feels herself falling asleep.

And she dreams about dark tunnels and strange men watching her.

Then she feels a sharp pain in her arm, and she almost screams.

She looks to see what the pain is and pulls her headphones from her ears.

"I'm sorry, dear," the old woman says, and Sarah sees that the woman's cloth bag is touching her arm. "Did I wake you up? It must be something in my bag. I have all my knitting things[2] in here." The old woman looks very upset[3] and apologetic[4].

"It's okay," Sarah says and smiles. "I was just surprised."

"Oh, you poor thing, you look exhausted. I'll move my bag so you can sleep."

"It's okay. I don't want to sleep."

"No, you relax," the old woman says, and Sarah thinks the old lady has a kind smile.

Sarah nods and is about to put her headphones back in her ears when she feels someone watching her, and she looks at the corner of the carriage.

The strange man, the man who looks like the evil character from her thriller; his eyes are open now.

And they are watching her.

She feels a cold shiver move over her body, and suddenly she thinks that she feels a little ill[5].

Is he watching her? She looks again and, yes, his hood is still covering his face, but she is sure that his eyes are focused on her.

---

1   **exhausted** – *erschöpft*
2   **knitting things** – *Strickzeug*
3   **upset** – *traurig*
4   **apologetic** – *entschuldigend*
5   **to feel ill** – *sich krank fühlen*

She tries to stay calm. There are still several people in the carriage: the young couple is still there and the two businessmen.

And the next station is North Acton, her station.

You just need to get home, she tells herself, and she feels the train slow down[1], and she knows she must get up.

"Is this your stop, dear?" the old woman asks.

Sarah nods.

"Oh, good. You're nearly home. Nearly time to get some sleep." Sarah tries to smile.

"Are you okay, dear? You look a little pale."

"Yes, just tired."

"You should put some water on your face. You'll feel better."

Sarah nods. "I will. Thank you."

I will, she thinks, but only if the strange man stays on the train. If he follows me, I will shout and scream for help.

She stands up and looks in the corner of the carriage one more time, but it looks like the man is asleep.

Go. Go now, she tells herself.

The doors open, and she quickly walks through them.

For a few seconds she walks and then turns back to look at the tube train. No one is there. No one gets off apart from her, she is sure.

The train starts again and she relaxes a little.

The platform at North Acton is quiet, but it always is at this time of the evening. She can see the stairs to the street, and she wants to walk to them, but she feels so weak.

She decides to go into the station toilets. All she needs is a little water.

She enters the ladies'[2] and stands in front of the mirror. Her arm hurts, so she takes her jacket off, and in the mirror she can see a small drop of blood on her skin.

---

1   **to slow down –** *bremsen*
2   **ladies'–** *Damentoilette*

"It's okay, dear, you will feel better in a moment. I gave you a little medicine to help you sleep."

Sarah jumps at the sound of the voice, and in the mirror she sees the reflection of the old woman. "What?" she tries to say, but then she falls to the floor. "Help me…" she says in a weak voice.

The old woman smiles, but it is a horrible smile. "I am helping you, dear. You poor thing. So tired, so exhausted. You can't live like that. But it's okay now: I'm here to help you."

And the old woman takes a long, thin knitting needle[1] from her bag, and Sarah remembers what the kid said on the tube…

… He uses something strange: not a knife but something long and thin, and he stabs them again and again, and they just bleed and bleed.

She tries to scream, but it is too late.

---

1   **knitting needle –** *Stricknadel*

The Tube, wie die Londoner ihre U-Bahn nennen, war die erste Untergrundbahn der Welt. Die Eröffnung des ersten Streckenabschnitts fand im Jahre 1863 statt. Lange hat die London Tube mit ihren 402 Kilometern den Rekord als längstes Streckennetz der Welt gehalten: Mittlerweile ist sie auf Platz drei hinter die U-Bahn-Netze von Shanghai und Peking gerutscht.

Eine Besonderheit des Londoner U-Bahn-Netzes ist, dass an den Haltestellen Personal zu finden ist, das u. a. den Fahrtgästen mit dem Kauf von Fahrtkarten an den Automaten hilft und Auskunft über den Fahrplan gibt.

Die London Tube dient aber nicht nur dem Personenverkehr: Während des Zweiten Weltkriegs wurden tief gelegene U-Bahn-Stationen als Luftschutzbunker benutzt. Außerdem trafen sich Premierminister Churchill und sein Kabinett in der heute geschlossenen Station Down Street.

WORTLISTE

Verwendete Abkürzungen

AE = amerikanisches Englisch
BE = britisches Englisch

AUS = australisches Englisch
ugs. = umgangssprachlich

	a pair of scissors	eine Schere	to	be aware	merken
	accelerator	Gaspedal	to	be fair	helles Haar haben
	ace	Ass	to	be scared	Angst haben
to	add	hinzufügen	to	be sore	weh tun
to	adjust	zurechtrücken; sich anpassen	to	be terrified	schreckliche Angst vor etw. haben
	advice	Ratschlag		bearded	bärtig
	alive with	voller	to	beat	besiegen
	All rise!	Bitte erheben Sie sich!		because of	wegen
			to	beg	anflehen
	almost	fast		behind	Hintern
	amazement	Erstaunen		belly	Magen
	amount	Summe	to	belong	gehören
	annoyed	genervt, verärgert		beneath	darunter
	anything but	nichts anderes als		billboard	Reklametafel
	apologetic	entschuldigend		blindfold	Augenbinde
to	apologise	um Entschuldigung bitten		bloke	(AUS, BE) Kerl
				bloody	(AUS, BE) verdammt
	appendix	Blinddarm			
	as	während	to	blush	erröten
	at first	zuerst		body	Leiche
	atmospheric	stimmungsvoll		bored	gelangweilt
	attendant	Wärter		boring	langweilig
	awake	munter	to	bother	stören
	awkward silence	betretenes Schweigen		brave	mutig
			to	bray	wiehern, kreischen
	badge with her name	Namensschild	to	brew	brauen
				brick	Baustein
	bald	kahl		brief	kurz
	bang	Knall		bright	intelligent
	bank robbery	Banküberfall		buck	(AE, ugs.) Dollar
	baseball bat	Baseballschläger		building work	Bauarbeiten
to	be about to do sth.	im Begriff sein, etw. zu tun		bullet	Patrone
				burglar	Einbrecher(in)
to	be asleep	schlafen		buried	begraben

	cabin	Hütte
	cannot help but	nicht umhin kommen, etw. zu tun
	carefully	vorsichtig; aufmerksam
	carriage	Wagen
	casual	locker
to	catch	fangen
	chamber	Amtskammer
to	chase	verfolgen
to	cheat	schummeln
to	cheer	jubeln
	chest	Brust
	chief inspector	Hauptkommissar
	chipped and bitten	eingerissen und abgekaut
to	chop	hacken
	class	Unterricht
	clearing	Waldlichtung
	club	Knüppel
	collar	Kragen
	comforting	beruhigend
to	commit a crime	ein Verbrechen begehen
	common thief	gemeiner Dieb
	commuter	Pendler
	companion	Begleiter(in)
	comparison	Vergleich
	complexion	Teint
	comprehensive school	≈ Gesamtschule
	concerned	besorgt
	concrete	Beton
to	confess	beichten
	confession	Geständnis
	confessional	Beichtstühl
	confused	irritiert
to	consider	überlegen
	content	zufrieden
	control panel	Bedienungspult
	cop	(AE) Bulle
	coroner	Gerichtsmediziner
	cosy	gemütlich
	counter	Schalter
	couple	Paar
	court clerk	Gerichtsdiener
	courtroom	Gerichtssaal
	courtyard	Innenhof
	coz	(ugs.) weil
	crazy	verrückt
	creek	Nebenfluss

to	creep	sich schleichen
	crime	Verbrechen
	crime novel	Kriminalroman
	crowd (of people)	Menschenmenge
	cruel	grausam
	cruise	Kreuzfahrt
	cry	Schrei
to	cry out	schreien
	customs	Zoll
to	dare	wagen
	darkness	Dunkelheit
	dear	Schatz
	deceased	verstorben
	deck of cards	Kartenset
	deer	Reh
	defeated	besiegt
	defence	Verteidigung
	defence	Strafverteidiger
	defendant	Angeklagter
	deserted	verlassen
	desperately	verzweifelt
	despite	trotz
to	destroy	vernichten
to	detect	entdecken
to	dig up	ausgraben
to	disappear	verschwinden
	distraction	Ablenkung
	Do you mind?	Stört es Sie?
	donkey	Esel
	doorway	Eingang
to	doubt	bezweifeln
	dressing gown	Bademantel
	driveway	Auffahrt
	due to	infolge
	dumb	(AE) dumm
	edge	Rand
	editor	Herausgeber(in)
	either... or	entweder... oder
to	empty	entleeren
	enemy	Feind
	enough	genug
to	enter a property by force	einbrechen
to	escape	fliehen
	evidence	Beweis
	except for	bis auf
	exhausted	erschöpft
to	expect	erwarten
	expression	Gesichtsausdruck
	expressionless	ausdruckslos
	extremely	äußerst

to	fade	schwinden	to	growl	anknurren
	fake	falsch		guard	garda, Polizist(in)
to	fall asleep	einschlafen		guilt	Schuldgefühl
	familiar	vertraut		guy	Kerl
	fan	Lüfter		hare	Hase
	fault	Schuld	to	hate	hassen
	fear	Angst	to	have to agree	zugeben müssen
	feeding frenzy	Futterstreit		He seems to	Er scheint diese
to	feel ill	sich krank fühlen		like that bag	Tasche sehr
to	feel sympathy	mit jdm. Mitleid		very much.	zu mögen.
	for sb.	haben	to	head for sth.	auf etw. zugehen
to	fight	kämpfen		headmaster	Schulleiter
	figure	Gestalt		heartbroken	untröstlich
to	fire	abfeuern	to	hesitate	zögern
	fire engine	Feuerwehrauto		highway	Schnellstraße
	flare	Leuchtfackel	to	hike	wandern
	flask	Flachmann		hillside	Berghang
to	flee	flüchten	to	hit	schlagen
	footstep	Schritt		honest	ehrlich;
	Forestry	zuständige			aufrichtig
	Commission	Behörde für		hood	Kapuze
		die Forstwirt-	to	hop	springen
		schaft		horrible	schrecklich
	forgiveness	Vergebung	to	hunt	jagen
	foul	grauenhaft	to	hurt sb.	jdm. wehtun
	front desk	Empfang		I see.	Ich verstehe.
	fry (French fry)	(AE) Pommes		I suppose	wir können wohl...
	G'day!	(AUS) Hallo!		we can...	
to	gag	knebeln		icicle	Eiszapfen
	gagged	geknebelt		If you have to.	Wenn du musst.
	gambling city	Glücksspielstadt		impressive	imposant
	garbage	(AE) Abfall		in a sane state	zurechnungsfähig
	gardai	die irische Polizei		of mind	
	gently	vorsichtig		in a split second	im Bruchteil einer
to	get	(BE, ugs.)			Sekunde
		verstehen		in disbelief	ungläubig
to	get hurt	verletzt werden		in fact	eigentlich
to	get the hell out	aus dieser Stadt		infatuation	Vernarrtheit
	of this city	abhauen		injury	Verletzung
	giant	Riese		ink	Tinte
to	go for a pint	auf ein Bier gehen		innocent	unschuldig
to	go wrong	schiefgehen		instead	stattdessen
	Good Lord!	Du meine Güte!		insulted	beleidigt
	gossip	Tratsch	to	intend to	beabsichtigen,
	gown	Talar			vorhaben
to	grab	sich etw.		intruder	Einbrecher(in)
		schnappen		It feels like...	Es fühlt sich an
	grammar school	≈ Gymnasium			wie...
	granddad	Opa		jetty	Pier
	grille	Gitter		journey	Fahrt
to	groan	stöhnen	to	judge	beurteilen
	grounds	Anlagen	to	kick	treten

to	kick open the door	die Tür eintreten
to	kneel down	niederknien
	knitting needle	Stricknadel
	knitting things	Strickzeug
	lad	(BE) Kumpel
	ladder	Leiter
	ladies'	Damentoilette
	landing	Treppenabsatz
	last	zum letzten Mal
to	laugh at sb.	jdn. auslachen
	laughter	Gelächter
	lazy	faul
to	leave	verlassen
	leaves	Laub
to	let go of sth.	etw. loslassen
to	let sb. know	jdm. Bescheid geben
	licence	Führerschein
to	lie	liegen
to	load	laden
	loch	See
to	look for sth.	nach etw. suchen
to	lose one's mind	den Verstand verlieren
	lumber yard	Holzlager
	lump	Beule
	luv	Schatz (Kosename)
	magician	Zauberer
	magnificent	grandios
to	make	verdienen
to	make a fist	eine Faust machen
to	make notes	Notizen machen
to	make sb.'s hair stand up	jdm. die Haare zu Berge stehen lassen
to	make sure	sich vergewissern
to	make sure that...	dafür sorgen, dass...
to	manage to do sth.	es schaffen, etw. zu tun
	manslaughter	Totschlag
	marble	Marmor
to	match	passen
	mate	(AUS, BE) Kumpel
	mental	übergeschnappt
	miraculously	wie durch ein Wunder
	missing person	vermisste Person
	mistake	Fehler
	mood	Laune

	moor	Heideland
	muddy stain	Schlammfleck
	muscly	muskelbepackt
	neither... nor	weder... noch
	news headline	Schlagzeile
to	nod	mit dem Kopf nicken
	noise	Geräusch
	not a soul	keine Menschenseele
	not to be supposed to	nicht dürfen
	notepad	Notizblock
	nothing but	nichts außer
to	notice	merken
	nowhere near closed	längst nicht abgeschlossen
	NYPD	die New Yorker Polizei
	oak	Eiche
	oar	Ruder
to	observe	beaobachten
	occasionally	gelegentlich
	ocean liner	Ozeandampfer
	Oh boy!	Junge, Junge!
	Oh my!	Meine Güte!
	onlooker	Betrachter
	ordinary	herkömmlich
	paint	Lack
	pale	hell, blass
	parish church	Pfarrkirche
	park ranger	Parkaufseher
to	pass away	entschlafen
to	pass by	vorbeigehen
	patiently	geduldig
	pew	Kirchenbank
to	pick	auswählen
to	pick up	aufheben
	pickup truck	Geländewagen
	picture	Foto
	piece of cloth	Stoffstück
	plain	Ebene
	plates	Nummernschild
to	play it straight	ehrlich sein
to	poach	wildern
to	point to sth.	auf etw. zeigen
	polish	Politur
	pom	(AUS, abwertend) Brite
	premeditated murder	Mord
	premises	Grundstück

	pride	Stolz		savage	brutal
	prisoner	Gefangener		scaffolding	Baugerüst
to	promise	versprechen	to	scare sb.	jdn. erschrecken
	prosecution	Staatsanwalt-schaft		scarecrow	Strohmann
				scared	verängstigt, ängstlich
to	prove	beweisen			
	puff	Atemstoß		scent	Duft
to	pull shut	zuziehen		school tie	Krawatte der Schuluniform
to	punish	bestrafen			
	push	Stoß, Schubs	to	seem	scheinen
	quiet	still		sensation	Gefühl
	rabbit	Kaninchen		sensible question	vernünftige Frage
to	raise	heben			
	raw	wund	to	separate	trennen
to	reach	erreichen		serious trouble	große Schwierig-keiten
to	reach sth. out to sb.	jdm. etw. hinstrecken			
to	reach up to	bis... hinauf-reichen	to	shake one's head	den Kopf schütteln
	real	echt		shape	Zustand; Gestalt
to	realise	merken, feststellen		shark	Hai
				sharp pain	stechender Schmerz
to	recall sth.	sich an etw. erinnern			
				shift	Schicht
to	reckon	meinen		shiver	Schauder
	recording device	Aufnahmegerät	to	shoot	schießen
			to	shoot sb.	jdn. erschießen
to	refill sb.'s glass	jdm. nach-schenken		shot	Schrot; Schuss
				should	sollten
	reflection	Spiegelbild		shout	lauter Ruf
	registration	Kraftfahrzeugbrief	to	shout	rufen
	relief	Erleichterung	to	show sb. out	jdn. hinaus-begleiten
	remote	abgelegen			
to	reply	antworten	to	shrug	mit den Achseln zucken
to	rescue	retten			
	rifle	Gewehr	to	shuffle	mischen
to	rock	schaukeln		shyly	schüchtern
	roof	Dach		sigh	Seufzen
	rope	Seil	to	sigh	seufzen
to	rot	verfaulen		silly	albern
	routine check	Routinekontrolle	to	sink	versinken
to	row	rudern		Sir?	Wie, bitte?
	rubbish	(BE) Müll		skyscraper	Wolkenkratzer
	rubbish collector	Müllabfuhrwagen	to	slap	ohrfeigen
				sleeping pill	Schlaftablette
	rude	unhöflich	to	slide open	aufschieben
	rules and regulations	Regeln und Vorschriften	to	slow down	bremsen
				snap	Schuss, Schnapp-schuss, Foto
to	rumble	knurren			
	saltie	australisches Leistenkrokodil		sneaker	(AE) Turnschuh
				solitary	einsam
				spare money	erübrigtes Geld
	sanctuary	Zuflucht		spare room	Gästezimmer

to	speak up	lauter sprechen
to	speed	flitzen
to	spot sth. from a mile away	sofort erkennen
to	spread	sich ausbreiten
to	stab sb.	jdn. niederstechen
to	stay awake	munter bleiben
to	stay cool	ruhig bleiben
to	steal	stehlen
	steering wheel	Lenkrad
to	step onto	betreten
	stomach	Bauch
	strangely	seltsam
	strap	Riemen
to	stretch out	sich ausstrecken
	stubby	(AUS) Bier
	suddenly	plötzlich
to	suggest	vorschlagen
	suit	Anzug
to	suit sb.	jdm. stehen
to	suppose	vermuten
to	suppress the image	die Vorstellung unterdrücken
	surface	Oberfläche
to	surround	umgeben
	suspect	Verdächtige(r)
	suspicion	Verdacht
to	swallow	schlucken
	sweat	Schweiß
to	swing	schwingen
to	take a deep breath	tief einatmen
	tartan	schotten- gemustert
	terraced house	Reihenhaus
	terrible reputation	schlechter Ruf
	terrifyingly	erschreckend
to	testify	aussagen
	Thames	die Themse
	the outback	Hinterland Australiens
	the sun sets	die Sonne geht unter
	this is it	jetzt oder nie
	though	jedoch, obwohl
	threatening	bedrohend
	thunder	Donner
to	tie	fesseln
	tied	gebunden

	tied to	angebunden an
	topic	Thema
	trace	Spur
to	trace	nachverfolgen
	track	Spur
	transfer	Überweisung
	trouble	Ärger
	trunk	(AE) Kofferraum
	tube	Londoner U-Bahn
to	tumble	fallen
	twist	Wendung
	uncommon	ungewöhnlich
	unfortunately	bedauerlicher- weise, leider
	unkind	unfreundlich
	unless...	es sei denn, ...
	upper sixth form	≈ gymnasiale Oberstufe
	upset	traurig
	van	Lieferwagen
	verdict	Urteilsspruch
	vibrant	lebendig
	victim	Opfer
	victorious	siegreich
	visible	sichtbar
	waist	Taille
	wardrobe	Kleiderschrank
	waste of time	Zeitverschwen- dung
	waterfalls	Wasserfälle
	weak	schwach
	weapon	Waffe
to	wear	tragen
	weird	seltsam
	wet	nass, feucht
	Whoah!	Langsam!
	wig	Perücke
	wire	Draht
to	wonder	sich fragen, sich wundern
	wooden	hölzern
	workman	Handwerker
to	worry	sich Sorgen machen
	worse	schlimmer
to	wrap	wickeln, umwickeln
	wuss	Weichei
	You got it.	Genau!
	You got it?	Alles klar?

WORTLISTE